REFRAME & RECLAIM

A 7-Step Guide to REFRAME Your Relationship with Your Belongings & RECLAIM Your Space

Jennifer Harris &
Courtney Huckabay, M.Ed, LPC-S, NCC

Copyright © 2024
Jennifer Harris & Courtney Huckabay, M.Ed, LPC-S, NCC

Performance Publishing
McKinney, TX

All Worldwide Rights Reserved.

All rights reserved. No part of this publication may be reproduced, stored in a retrieval system or transmitted, in any form or by any means, electronic, mechanical, recorded, photocopied, or otherwise, without the prior written permission of the copyright owner, except by a reviewer who may quote brief passages in a review.

ISBN: 978-1-961781-60-3 (paperback)
ISBN: 978-1-961781-68-9 (ebook)

INTRODUCTION

Jennifer

October 2, 2021, was the twenty-fifth anniversary of my father's passing. This day also happened to be the day my family and I were helping my brother prepare for a new chapter in his life. My brother was making space for a new roommate, and we spent the weekend moving furniture and reorganizing his home. As we sifted through his belongings, we came across sentimental items that my brother kept from childhood.

Being reminded of our past memories, I found myself in a state of reflection and self-analysis. At forty years old, time seemed to pass so quickly. It was hard to believe my father was not present for most of my life and many significant milestones. My brother held onto so many items that reminded him of childhood that I wondered if he kept these items so he would not forget the past, the same reason I chose to keep my childhood belongings. We were both well into our adulthood, however, our homes reflected much of our past.

My brother and his kids lived in a 2400-square-foot home, with a majority of the bookshelves and wall space covered with memorabilia, collectibles, and memories of joyous times. As we began to sort, organize, and decipher what items to keep, categorize, and discard, he was challenged to let go of multiple things. Most every item in his home brought a smile to his face when he discussed the story behind the object and remembered the past.

However, with the addition of a new roommate sharing this four-bedroom, three-bath home, it was apparent some of his belongings needed to be filtered and let go of to make room and available space for everyone to live in it comfortably. How could his current home allow for another person with their possessions to fill more of his home's real estate? Each item my brother agreed to keep in his possession gave him joy, but to someone else who did not have the emotional attachment to the items, most of his belongings were just "stuff." The belongings that occupied his home were fun and memorable items, not necessarily junk; however, not all of the objects were meeting the needs and wants of his current home and his current chapter of life.

As we continued to work our way through each room filled with more possessions, I began to realize it was difficult for him to part with these objects. Every item brought forth an emotional response – Items that were joyful reminders of childhood, an abundance of useful items, and even random scraps of items that might come in handy one day. For me, most of these things were just "stuff." I had no emotional tie to these items. It would be easy for me to let go of them, but for him, there were deep emotional attachments. From my perspective, the value placed on the many possessions in his home seemed to steal and suffocate the functionality of his home. The reluctance to let go of some of the items in his home created an obstacle to prepare for the next chapter of his life.

As I took inventory of his home, I began to reflect on the countless boxes of sentimental items that had taken up space *in my own home* for years. If someone walked through my home, my belongings would also just be "stuff" that others could easily discard. Like my brother, my strong emotional ties to my things created the excuses I told myself so that I felt justified to keep items that no longer serve me in my present lifestyle. In reality, it was not only the physical space that the boxes occupied in my home, but the mental and emotional space the boxes took up in my mind was overwhelming as well.

As we continued to take inventory of his home, the kitchen mirrored the same mentality that had plagued my grandparents during their lifetime. My grandfather died when I was nine years old, and my grandmother was diagnosed with Alzheimer's a few years later. I have only a few memories of my time with my grandparents, but one of the most prevalent memories is of my grandfather's workshop in the basement of his home. There were boxes and boxes of random bits and bobs, cardboard scraps, Styrofoam, paperclips, fabric remnants, and miniature knick-knacks galore. In retrospect, you could see the lasting effects of living through the Great Depression. The notion to keep everything for fear of being without was apparent in the items he stored in the basement. I wondered if my brother and I both saw how my grandfather lived and adopted those learned habits even though we have never experienced a time of scarcity.

I collected knick-knacks and decorative items to display in my home while my brother bought in oversized bulk and kept most things – "just in case." For instance, he had easily over thirty coffee mugs. Now, he does drink large amounts of coffee and does host many friends and family at his home, but I cannot recall a time that he had thirty people over for coffee at one time. Another cabinet overflowed with multiple sizes of free to-go disposable plastic cups. When I asked him why he needed so many cups his response was, "You always need a good large plastic cup."

As the conversations continued during the house reorganization, more patterns and justifications emerged.

Me: "Can we throw away these scraps of wood?"

My brother (jokingly but stil not willing to part with the pile of wood): "Do you know how expensive wood is? That could cover my retirement. It would be a better return on investment than leaving my money in a savings account."

Me: "How many eggs are in the fridge?"
Brother: "Four dozen."
Me: "Do you eat them all?"
Brother: "Yes."
Me: "Your fridge is not large enough to accommodate all those eggs with all your other food. Is it really worth the savings of buying in bulk if you have to play Tetris every time you open the fridge or your pantry? Even if you're sharing food with your new roommate, they will want to have a place to put their food."

He then glared at me with a look that said, *You might have a point, but I like doing things this way.*

(To his credit, my brother does not typically waste the food he purchases in bulk; however, his home is not designed to store the amount of bulk food he attempts to store. And while everything fits behind the closed cabinets and refrigerator doors, once the doors are opened, it becomes a challenge to retrieve and return items from the back of the overfilled shelves. There is so much stored in the space allotted that the inability to access and navigate the items in the space hinders its functionality and flow.)

Patterns emerged within the habits of my own family, including myself. I stepped back and began thinking about my family's history and how we came to be so tied to our stuff: the bulk items at my brother's house, the countless "treasures" that were passed down to my mother from her parents, and the sentimental items I kept from loved ones who had passed. As I dove deeper into reflection, several patterns of excuses became highlighted. These justifications were keeping me from discarding items that were taking up valuable real estate in my mind and home. These following excuses were reflected in many of my personal reasons for keeping things.

Utilitarian
"YOU CAN NEVER HAVE TOO MANY."
"I MAY NEED IT OR USE IT ONE DAY."

Value
"IT'S SUCH A GOOD DEAL."
"IT HAS VALUE."

Sentiment & Remembrance
"BUT IT WAS A GIFT."
"IT'S SENTIMENTAL."

Lifestyle & Hobbies
"BUT IT BRINGS ME JOY."
"I'M A COLLECTOR; IT'S FOR MY COLLECTION."

I then dove deeper and asked myself:

- *Are the boxes and shelves of clutter worth the mental toll of keeping each and every item that triggers a memory?*
- *Why do we, as humans, put such an emphasis on holding so tightly to our stuff that it takes away from our home's functionality?*
- *If we store an item in the garage and don't see it every day, is this a good enough reason to continue to allow it to take up physical real estate?*
- *What creates our emotional tie to our stuff?*
- *Why do we keep items that once had value but are no longer helpful in the present?*

So I asked my friend Courtney, who is a mental health professional, to give me possible perspectives I was noticing in myself and my family. As we talked, I realized that my family is not unique in the fact that we have learned to attach ourselves to our belongings. Our possessions are tangible items that connect us to our memories and help us to solidify our identity. Courtney gave me some interesting insight into this phenomenon.

Courtney

People of all cultures and generations find their identity and value through the things that they possess, collect, and use. A farmer can be more productive and efficient with his farming tools and machines. A teacher can reach more young minds with the books and school supplies to educate and create. How do we find our own identity in things?

- *As a mother, are we inclined to keep our children's newborn outfit worn home from the hospital?*
- *As a novice competitor, are we expected to collect the baseball cards that inspired our talents and efforts to be an athlete?*
- *As an artist, must I create and mold beautiful masterpieces to only keep them stored away in a basement for my eyes only?*
- *How much stuff do we need to collect to validate our significance in our world while being content to live a life with meaning and purpose?*

Objects and belongings connect us to our identity, whether cultural, familial, religious, career, etc. Parting ways with objects can, at times, create a feeling of distance and separation from whom we identify ourselves as and our communities that we identify with; however, this is only a mental state of separation. Our actual identity lies within our understanding of who we are, not in the objects we own or possess. Finding validation and assurance in our personal identity is the sole responsibility of each individual – for themselves.

Pairing down our belongings and possessions can be a challenging feat for many. Defining the value of our own possessions – which ones to keep and cherish and others to release from our ownership – is subjective to each individual. Many can place a monetary value on some items; however, other material possessions only have a value to their rightful owner. The value comes solely from the owner's personal perspective and valuation of each possession. Editing our belongings and possessions can also be an exercise of clarity, value, and freedom for many.

We all have road blocks in our lives that have mentally kept us from moving forward into our optimal mental space and ideal physical environment. Some are unaware of the effects that our home environments have on our mental space or mental load; however, many realize the toll that disorganization, clutter, and overwhelmed spaces have on their mood and overall mindset. Many can feel stuck and frozen in the stuff, unable to know where or how to begin the process of reclaiming their mental state and physical real estate.

This is more common than people realize. Others may have become accustomed to the lifestyle that has been created by disorganization and overcrowded spaces and feel apathetic to change. Every individual must navigate their own personal journey to reframe their connection to their possessions and reclaim the functionality of their personal environment.

* * * * *

HOW TO NAVIGATE THIS BOOK FOR YOUR PERSONAL JOURNEY

The mission of this book is to help people reframe their attachment to physical items and reclaim their mental, emotional, and physical real estate. This means becoming unstuck from unhelpful and unhealthy patterns in order to travel through life with authentic joy and freedom.

In each chapter, Jennifer shares her personal journey with each excuse and how she justifies storing items in her home. In the Reframe of each chapter, Courtney explores the mindset and psychology surrounding each justification, giving insight to the habits and systems that create challenges for so many people and their relationship to their belongings. Case studies with real-life clients are then detailed for you to witness the seven-step Reframe and R.E.C.L.A.I.M. process and to observe how this practice transforms each client's mindset and relationship with their belongings to improve the functionality of their physical space.

At the end of each chapter, questions are posed for you to reflect and evaluate your own personal journey with physical items. These questions can help you begin your personal journey to reframe and reclaim your mental, emotional, and physical real estate for a healthier life balance and improved peace of mind. The experiences and opinions explored in this book are relative to each individual. We hope you find guidance in how to navigate your own personal attachment to material things that can help you along your own personal journey.

> "One's destination is never a place, but rather a new way of seeing things."
> – Henry Miller

* * * * *

Jennifer

Growing up, my family loved a good road trip. And just like any road trip, your vehicle size determines how much stuff you can bring. Now, as my husband can attest, I can Tetris a week's worth of "essentials" for a two-day trip but in reality, no one wants to travel cross country with luggage on their lap and things piled up so high that the driver cannot see out of the rear view mirror. Besides, the more open space you have while traveling, the more comfortable you will be, the easier it will be to find the items you have along the way, and the easier it will be to see the beautiful scenery surrounding you.

In essence, the same theory applies to our homes, or our real estate. The amount of real estate you have will dictate how much stuff you can potentially fill inside of your space. While maxing out our space in our home is not the goal, this tends to be the trend in our homes. Almost subconsciously, we think that the larger my physical real estate is, the more things I can stuff inside of it.

Imagine this book as a road trip metaphor. Life is a journey – a road trip of sorts. On our life's journey, we collect experiences, material objects, and memories along the way. Knowing what to pack, what route to take to our next destination, and realizing what roadblocks keep us stuck in life can be challenging.

Every chapter will take you through a personal mission to reflect, evaluate, and take action to eliminate the excuses that create roadblocks. Some chapters will take longer than others based on your own life experiences and personal mindset; however, we must remember that it is impossible to keep every memento we encounter on our road trip and still manage to fit everything in our vehicle comfortably along the journey of our life.

As we move from one destination to another, we will reflect, evaluate, and reframe what we want to keep packed in our bags and what we want to unpack and release. This will allow for a continued life journey with enough "space" to focus on living life to the fullest, acquiring more memories, and reclaiming our mental and physical real estate.

So let's unpack our bags together. I'll go first.

CHAPTER 1

DISCOVERING WHAT IS REALLY IMPORTANT

Jennifer

Don't look now, but your house is on fire! I am sure you did not think a book about organization was going to start so intensely. Okay, so your house is not really on fire, but let us reflect on the great wisdom you can draw from hypotheticals. All of your loved ones, including human and furry, are safe, and you have collected all the important documents needed. What are the three items you rescue?

Now, imagine that you've grown four extra arms and have super strength. You can now carry an additional three items. What are all of the things you chose to rescue from your home? Now, to be honest, how many of these chosen items do you know exactly where they are and are easily accessible if this hypothetical were to occur?

These are the questions I have asked myself to understand what I truly use and value in my home. When I start evaluating items and spaces I want to declutter, I often find myself justifying my decisions to keep items based on the excuse that I have the physical space to store items. Therefore, I do nothing but procrastinate in my decision making. I even purchased a home with a three-car garage hoping that this would finally solve my clutter and storage problems; however, this attempted solution only grew the allowable space for me to add more stuff to my home.

When I choose these justifications to keep items rather than evaluating my relationship with my belongings, I interfere with the functionality and flow of my home and my desired lifestyle. I continue on this procrastination loop because it is easier to ignore the problem that my stuff creates than to make the difficult decisions surrounding my relationship with stuff. Instead, I am choosing to live in a space that does not optimally function and continues to be a burden. I am choosing to add financial stress by repeatedly relocating boxes when I move from home to home. I am choosing to live with the mental distress of visual clutter and creating emotional stress for my family members. I am also choosing to be wasteful when I keep an item that I may possibly use one day instead of passing it on to someone that can use it today. Again, the mental load, physical space, and emotional conflict I hold continue to be a burden to me and my home.

In 2020, fear and uncertainty spread throughout the world with the COVID-19 pandemic. We did not know what this new illness meant for ourselves, our families, or our world. It seemed as if so much was out of our control. As I sat in my home with all of my thoughts and all of my things, I went down a rabbit hole. What can I do to protect my family and my home? What items do I need for survival? What items do I hold the closest to my heart?

I quickly realized that my sentimental Barbie collection I had been hauling around for the past twenty years was not going to help me survive in life, nor would I grab this collection if my house was burning down. So why was it so important to carry the physical, financial, and mental burden of storing these items for twenty years? Why did I initially keep the items? Originally, I wanted to keep them because I had such fond memories of playing with them, and if I ever had a girl, she could play with them as well.

My mother kept some toys from her childhood and I always enjoyed carefully looking at them. I saw the joy in her eyes as she recalled stories from her childhood. The major difference from my mother's collection of childhood toys and my collection was the amount of toys she kept. My mother had a Chatty Cathy doll and two Barbies with a few outfits in a carrying case. I, on the other hand, kept all of my Barbies from childhood, including the Barbie ice cream store, the Barbie airplane, the Barbie bathtub, the Barbie & the Rockers' stage, her giraffe, and the Barbie convertible home-to-office playset. This collection filled two large storage bins, and I have only opened them twice in the past twenty years. In reflection, *How much do I truly value this collection that I store in my 110 degree or hotter Texas garage?*

As I reflected on what I truly valued, I realized that the items that have the most value and bring me joy are my countless photos that hold the precious images of family members; however, if there were a disaster or if I needed to quickly evacuate, it would be impossible for me to quickly find and take the several boxes of photos buried at the bottom of my entertainment center. After this realization, I needed to find a solution to ease my anxiety and worry. I remedied this issue by purchasing an external hard drive and a digital scanner to scan all of my physical photos. Now I store the external hard drive in my fireproof safe with all of my other important documents in the event that there is a home disaster. Now, I can realistically evacuate and take my important photos with me. The best part about this solution is I am able to continue to store as many images as I want without the guilt of using valuable space in my home as storage. Now that my concerns about my photographs have been resolved, my peace of mind is restored.

When reflecting on your personal belongings, how many of the items that reside in your home would you realistically replace if they were lost or damaged in a fire or natural disaster? According to the *LA Times* and NAPO (National Association of Professional Organizers), the average home contains 300,000 items of which we only use about twenty percent. How many items are you holding on to because you tell yourself you have the space to keep them even though you are not using these items? How much physical space might you reclaim in your home if you chose to remove eighty percent of the things in your home that you do not use? How much physical space would you be able to enjoy if you simply went through your stuff and only kept what is really important to you rather than keeping things out of a sense of obligation, fear, or procrastination? How much value are the items in your home currently demanding from your physical real estate, mental and emotional resources, and financial assets?

* * * * *

In each chapter we will use the R.E.C.L.A.I.M. process to thoroughly examine our spaces. By REFRAMING our mindset and relationship surrounding our clutter, we are able to RECLAIM the real estate in our home that was previously used to store unused items. Remember that this is *your* process. Take your time and be honest with yourself. As you begin, follow the seven-step R.E.C.L.A.I.M. process below:

R – REFLECT on the current space. *How is it currently being used? What is your hope for the functionality of this space? What aesthetic do you hope to achieve in this space? How do you want to feel when you experience this space?*

E – EVALUATE each item and understand the true value each item has for you as you empty the space. Reimagine how this space functions. *How does each item fit into your aspirational space? Does each item belong in this new space's aesthetic and function that you have imagined?*

C – CLEAN the space. Empty and clean the space so that it feels like a fresh, clean slate. *How do you feel seeing this space empty versus how you felt with the space occupied with items?*

L – LAYOUT and label the space before placing items back into the space. Attempt to create a blueprint of how the space will look and feel. Measure and readjust the space to fit the space's new functionality, as well as any organizational materials that you may include to enhance the aesthetic and functionality.

A – ASSEMBLE items back into the space and adjust as needed. Allow for trial and error as you reimagine the space's blueprint. This may be adjusting materials, changing where items are located, or reframing what items are truly intended for this new environment.

I – INSPECT the space once everything is reassembled. Step back and take inventory, viewing the aesthetic and functionality of the newly reimagined space. This is the final gut check – *does this space now match the intention you imagined? Does this now fit your space's function and your current lifestyle needs?*

M – MAINTAIN your space. Remember that this space will only stay as organized and aesthetically pleasing as you put effort and intentionality into it. *What steps will you need to take to assure that this space will continue to function and feel like it does right now?* Create a plan and a system to purposefully maintain this new space, recruiting any other people needed that utilize or enjoy this space. Accountability is key.

Once you have given yourself time to live in the newly reclaimed space, be sure to allow yourself to reflect and reevaluate your space and its functionality as your lifestyle changes. If you find that this space is no longer meeting your lifestyle needs or you want to change the aesthetic or functionality of your space, start again with the seven steps of R.E.C.L.A.I.M. It is important to reevaluate your home's space as you continue on your life's journey. This is not a process that is complete in one round. Be flexible and adapt as you discover what works and what does not work for you and the space.

CHAPTER 2

YOU CAN NEVER HAVE TOO MANY

"Want a thingamabob? I've got twenty."
– Ariel

Jennifer

I love pillows and, in my world, *who doesn't love pillows?* They can easily be changed out with the season, they make a space feel warm, and they provide me with back support (especially the older I get). They are functional and beautiful and *you can never have too many!* However, the first thing my husband does before relaxing on the couch is remove the decorative pillows. Sometimes the pillows just get tossed to another section of the couch. At other times, they may be relocated to a different area in the room or even moved into another room altogether.

From his point of view, having the pillows costs him the physical time and the mental energy to move them from the space to fit his comfort level. From my point of view, when I come into my home and see the decorative pillows in disarray, it takes my physical time and mental energy to return them to their "rightful" place. This has become a daily ritual. My aesthetic need and comfort level versus his minimalistic needs for comfort create an environment that has yet to live up to its optimal function. While it may only take thirty seconds of time to relocate the pillows, this is time taken away from enjoying our home and time together.

This daily pillow routine is multiplied by my kids. For my boys, pillows are toys to play with, and of course, they never put them back to where they found them. I continually find my decorative pillows tossed about my home, and I go through the repeated frustration of picking up pillows multiple times a day. To really understand the true cost of these decorative pillows, that *only I* seem to appreciate on the sofa, I took a deep dive. I evaluated the physical and mental toll the pillows were taking on my family and myself. See below for the breakdown I used to truly understand the total cost of having all of my beautiful pillows.

THE TIME TOLL

I spend approximately ten minutes a week picking up and rearranging pillows. While it may not seem like much time, that turns into *520 minutes a year*. That is *eight hours and forty minutes* of time that I could be spending doing something else. Notice that I did not say it was wasted time. If the pillows bring me that much joy, and it does not bother me to pick them up from different areas in the house over and over again, then choosing to use my time in this manner is justified; however, if I would rather spend that time going for a walk or playing a game, then I need to take a step back and reframe my relationship with my pillows.

As a single woman without kids, I enjoyed my decorative and seasonal pillows. Once they were placed where I enjoyed them, they stayed in place. Little time was spent picking up pillows off of the floor or searching my space for a pillow that was misplaced. Therefore, the aesthetic payoff was worth the little time I invested. Instead of my time being spent on pillow arrangements, I spent my time on other priorities such as spending time with friends and family and relaxing in my comfortable home that was reflective of each season.

However, as my lifestyle has changed as a wife and a mother, so have my priorities. For my current chapter of life, I value spending more time with my family than rearranging my pillows. I continue to love my decorative pillows, but I also love quality time with my family, and my family does not love my pillows like I do. With self-reflection and some honest insight, I have learned to reframe my relationship with my decorative pillows and to choose family time over the stress of perfectly placed pillows on my sofa. One day, when my boys are no longer living in my home, I may return to my seasonal pillow rotation. This year, I choose to claim my 520 minutes with my family.

THE MENTAL TOLL

The smaller mental toll of owning all of my pillows is the brief annoyance I feel when I see the large pile of pillows taking up space in my garage. This irritation resurfaces each time I open the linen closet door to stuff the overflowing pillows back into place when they fall; however, both of these storage areas have doors I can close and hide away the clutter. This keeps these feelings at bay when these pillows are out of sight.

The larger mental cost and emotional toll is the daily frustration I feel when I have to pick up all of the pillows off the floor or rearrange them in an aesthetically pleasing style. When adding this mental cost to the other daily house chores, I realize that I would much rather spend my mental capacity on other things than pillow arrangements.

However, this does not account for the cost my husband was paying for these items he does not care for or value in our home. Honestly, at his core, my husband is a minimalist. He wants the sink kept empty at all times, countertops cleared off and decluttered, and everything to be tucked behind closed doors. He needs the visual clutter removed so he does not have to think about where to find things and can quickly see and find what he needs.

Unfortunately, he married an interior designer who is a recovering maximalist. It is easy for me to remember and identify where items are placed in our home among the intentionally designed spaces I create; however, the visual clutter causes my husband to misplace items he sets down among the "over designed" flat surfaces in our home. Needless to say, we have had some disagreements as to what is needed in our home to meet both of our mental and aesthetic desires. He becomes frustrated because he cannot quickly find items among the clutter, and I become frustrated because I am repeatedly spending my time helping him search the house for his misplaced items. At the end of the day, my husband and I are both mentally taxed.

THE REAL ESTATE TOLL

When my husband and I decided to marry, we chose to merge thirty-two years of my accumulated items and forty years of his accumulated items into a 1,900-square-foot home. Our items needed to create an environment where we both could function and thrive. As most combined households experience, we had several items that were duplicates and multiple items we both felt we could not part with. My husband had a much easier time parting with items, but soon our house became overwhelmed with the items that I had difficulty parting with. I had many excuses for why I needed to keep these items. Some items were sentimental and others I thought might be worth something someday. I found many items that I might use one day and others that just brought me joy. There was an emotional pull that made it difficult for me to make decisions, including my many pillows.

Currently, I have over twenty-five pillows separated by season, and I have compressed them as much as possible in vacuum sealed bags; however, they still take up a space of approximately four feet by three feet in my linen closet, and an additional four feet by two feet on a shelf in the garage. These are only the pillows that I store away during the offseason and these shelves do not include my collection of everyday pillows I place neatly on sofas, beds, and in window sills across my home. The combined space of the garage and linen closet equals approximately twenty square feet of storage for all of my offseason pillows.

Twenty square feet of space in a 1,900-square-foot home with a three-car garage may not seem like much, but that twenty square feet of space is allocated solely as storage for my pillows. When I combine all my beauty products, craft supplies, books, seasonal decorations, and childhood items, the storage space quickly adds up to several hundred square feet. I have attempted to set boundaries for myself and declared that 1,900 square feet is ample space for our family and our stuff. I will not take on the extra financial burden of paying for a storage unit, because I know I will rarely drive to the unit to retrieve my stored items. The unused items would sit there and waste away, becoming useless with age.

Therefore, I told myself that if I need more space than my home allocates, I need to declutter my items rather than devote more space to storage; however, upon honest self-reflection, my storage unit limits were being violated every day. Instead of using an offsite storage facility, my home and garage became the storage unit I swore I would never acquire. The overabundance of items in my garage, closets, cabinets, and bookshelves were being stored away, out of sight as if they were being stored in an offsite storage unit. I was wasting my home's real estate on items I was not using in my current chapter of life.

I had to take an honest look at my life and ask myself what I truly valued and how my home was reflecting those values.

Am I spending my time wisely by searching my home for misplaced items, or is my time better served spending it with my family? Was the function and utilization of the square footage of my home reflective of how I wanted my home environment to feel? I realized that by reducing the amount of real estate that my lesser-valued items occupied, I could help to increase the functionality of my home to meet my current lifestyle's values and goals.

For example, when I open my linen closet door, I currently prepare myself to dodge the precarious leaning tower of pillows on the top shelf that is destined to fall each time someone opens the closet door; however, If I limit my pillow storage space to one neatly organized lower shelf in the linen closet, I can alleviate the annoyance of the toppling pillows when I open the door. By doing this, I also have shelf space to fit my backstock toilet paper on the top shelf. Additionally, I will save time accessing my toilet paper in the linen closet, located next to the restroom, instead of walking all the way to my front hall closet where it is currently stored.

If I continue this momentum to R.E.C.L.A.I.M. other areas of my home, I could easily replace storing lower-valued items in the garage with parking my much higher-valued vehicle, reclaiming the garage storage to fit my current needs. The vehicle I use to safely transport my family has a much larger monetary and functional value, and I want to keep it protected from the elements and in top working condition. As I consider how much time, mental, and physical space these items were consuming of my home as a storage unit, I began to wonder the financial toll these low value items were costing me and my family.

THE FINANCIAL TOLL

I consider myself a thrifty shopper, and have purchased most of my pillows on discount; however, I have still spent over $500 on pillows over the years. In reflection, would I rather have *all* of these pillows, or would I rather have a couple of pillows and spend the remaining money on something I place more value in? For instance, the saved money could be spent on a swing for my front porch so I can watch my kids play as they grow up, or this money can go toward an experience on my ever growing bucket list of life. Again, there is no right or wrong answer, but personally, I value experiences over pillows today.

In addition to the money I spent to purchase items for my home, there is the hidden cost I pay in having a home large enough to store my belongings. The U.S. Census Bureau recorded that the median square footage of a new construction home in 2022 was 2,299 square feet, and the average size of the American home has nearly tripled in size over the past fifty years according to *NPR*.

Before writing this book, I had never acknowledged the excess and over consumption of my home because, in my eyes, everything fits in my modestly sized home; however, if I discarded or donated items that I no longer use, would I even need a 1,900-square-foot house? According to *Realtor.com* (March 2024), the median cost per square foot of a home in the United States is $228. If I could eliminate a hundred square feet of my home, I would save approximately $28,800. Then, I could pay off my mortgage a year sooner or go on several family trips.

Even if I did not downsize my home, the square footage that would be freed of the excess items would make my home feel less stressful and would reflect the feeling and values I want my home to possess. To me, that feeling alone is worth the cost per square foot to have the space decluttered and opened. Now, my intention is not to become a minimalist in my home design choices, but the intentional empty space would be more aesthetically pleasing and will make my home feel comfortable and complete.

Using the above statistic of $228 per square foot, I calculated the real estate toll of storing all of my extra pillows in my hallway linen closet. This total dollar value of space amounts to approximately $2,736 for twelve square feet of real estate in my linen closet to store my pillows. This became my *a-ha!* moment. When I reframe my mindset to consider the cost per square foot for my home storage, I am quickly able to evaluate and determine if the items I choose to keep in my home hold enough value to store them at $228 per square foot. This kind of math is rarely utilized to understand how your space is being used in dollar amounts; however, this can be shockingly insightful for anyone to calculate their own storage space figures.

Moving forward, when purchasing a new item for my home, I need to evaluate and classify how I personally value it compared to the financial cost for me to keep it in my home. Does the personal value I give each item justify the cost to my current lifestyle goals? Reframing our mindset of how our home functions and feels can create a new perspective of how your home is or is not functioning for yourself and your family.

REFRAME

"We have what we need, if we use what we have."
– Edgar Cahn

Courtney

The cost of storing personal items has become a fast growing industry. According to the Self Storage Association, in the United States alone, there are more than 50,000 storage facilities, amounting to approximately 7.3 square feet of storage space for every United States citizen. What does this statistic say about how we are utilizing the real estate in our homes? What is the true cost of arranging fifteen pillows on your family room couch? For some, it may seem insignificant, however, for others it is a massive mental, physical, and financial fee. Purchasing and storing pillows for each season of the year seems like a great idea until one must find the space to store these beautiful and fluffy home accessories. Where do these pillows reside when they are not on display? And when they are on display, does it add to the aesthetic and function of your home or take away? There is such a thing as too much of a good thing. But where does that line get drawn?

Depending on your personal real estate size and mental real estate capacity, too much of a good thing varies by individual. For some individuals who love redecorating and redesigning, too much is never enough. On the flip side, for those who are easily overstimulated or have difficulty with organization, only a few items can overwhelm the physical and mental space for that individual. We all have a limited amount of mental space and will power.

Self-awareness is an essential puzzle piece to finding the balance of aesthetic and function. What items bring joy and beauty to my personal space and how much stuff is enough or too much for the space? How does my own personal comfort compare to those that share the space with me? Simply put, what items do I need for my space to reflect me and be comfortable for me? According to the *Wall Street Journal*, Americans spend $1.2 trillion annually on nonessential goods or items that are not needed.

Knowing yourself and each member of your family's capacity for stuff is important. While flipping through a home magazine, do you feel overwhelmed or calm looking at the photos of living spaces? Do you have the mental capacity for continually redecorating and reorganizing your home or do you prefer more mental space for relaxing or focusing on other hobbies, needs, or wants? Self-awareness and positive and open communication are necessary to find the perfect balance of stuff for you and your family. Assuring that each individual in your home feels at home in the physical space is important. Transforming a house into a home includes meeting the wants and needs of those living in the home. Each person needs a space or spaces that reflect their personality and identity, within reason.

Imagine each individual having an emotional bank account. Each time that someone notices that you have a want or need and makes an effort to meet that need for you, a deposit is added. Each time that a need or want is ignored, a withdrawal is taken. Statistically, it takes five positive emotional deposits for each negative withdrawal for a relationship to remain healthy and positive. If we are not aware and willing to attempt to communicate, compromise, and meet our loved ones' needs, emotional bonds begin to break down and relationships can become distant or conflictual. Knowing what your mental and emotional capacity is for your space as well as the mental and emotional toll it takes on other family members in your home is paramount.

In addition, each family member needs to be reflected in the home. Displaying family photos, allowing children to have a voice in how their bedroom or playroom is decorated, and creating common areas that can be comfortable and lived in are different ways to ensure each individual has space in the home that reflects them. If you expect your home to be a museum, where nothing is to be touched or moved, it can create a physical environment of sterility and stress. On the other hand, if your home is a place of clutter and disarray, this can create a physical environment of stress and overstimulation. The goal is to find a healthy balance between your stuff and the space that it fills to create a comfortable and livable environment for everyone in the home.

When you survey your home, do the items in your home reflect you, your partner, and your children? Does your home feel like a space that is comfortable for you and each individual in your home? Allowing each individual to have input in the physical real estate of their space is important in helping each person feel included and validated in the home. Ideally, we all want our home to be functional, to feel safe and comfortable for everyone living in the home; however, we can get bogged down by our things and become stuck in a cluttered or dysfunctional physical space. This physical clutter can also create mental stressors and emotional distress for individuals living in the household.

The physical real estate, organization, and functionality of your home needs to meet the needs of your family as a whole, as well as meet the needs for each individual. It is important, but oftentimes challenging, to reflect and ask yourself questions to better understand yourself, the functionality of your real estate, and your family relationships that impact your home environment. Physically overfilling your home can cause emotional distress and relational conflict for families. What people do when their stuff cannot fit in their home, typically, is to purchase extra storage. According to *The New York Times Magazine*, one in ten Americans rent an offsite storage unit.

How much stuff do we need to feel like ourselves? Everyone has an identity; however, these identities shift and evolve overtime. We are not the same person we were when we were ten years old – nor is it healthy to try to be that same person. Life experiences and life lessons allow us to evolve into a different version of ourselves. Of course, we hope that these are wiser and more improved selves as we experience life and learn more about ourselves and our world. Unfortunately, we all can find ourselves stuck in life and feeling unsure of who we are or who we want to be. Accumulating things can reinforce or allow us to create the identity we want others to see.

My things are not me, and I am not my things; however, accumulating things to help reflect our personal identity is a slippery slope. Collecting things to validate our personal values and self-worth can create a false sense of security. Believing that our value and worth are only measured by our possessions and belongings is a fixed mindset. This mindset reinforces that our identity, how we see ourselves and possibly how others see us, is solely connected to what things I have in my possession. However, our identity is formed by much more than physical stuff. Our personality, our habits, our talents, our imperfections, and the challenges we overcome are a deeper definition of our true identity. Measuring our identity solely on what things we own or acquire is a shallow and fragile self-concept. If an unfortunate natural disaster were to destroy these physical belongings, who would we remain to be without them? This is a reframe of mindset that can help us to establish a deeper self-identity.

According to *Psychology Today*, Americans spend more on shoes, jewelry, and watches ($100 billion) than on higher education. Materialism and consumerism has created a culture that values consumption and spending over education and personal growth. Additionally, a Gitnux Marketdata Report in 2024 claims that twenty-two percent of Americans reported feeling pressured to buy things they did not need. So how many pillows, watches, tools, clothes, or toys do I need to feel like me? How much stuff do I need to validate who I am in this world? When is it too much of a good thing?

Consumerism in our current society has skyrocketed. Compared to fifty years ago, Americans are consuming twice as many material goods today according to *The Story of Stuff*. Now, this is a deeper topic that can be challenging to explore by reading this book alone. Consumerism is a complex topic with various positive outcomes for commerce and economic growth; however, this can also lead to burdens and financial challenges to the individual with the ideals of keeping up with the Joneses. We do encourage everyone to find time for reflection and self-awareness of your personal spending habits and relationship with stuff. This may be simply thinking back on your past and current habits or seeking out support from a professional mental health therapist to find improved self-awareness.

Finding time to reflect on your personal perspective, mindset, and emotional connection to your belongings and how they affect your physical space is important. Just like we grow and change with time, our space needs to reflect that change. Although this process can be challenging, allowing your space to change and evolve with your family's identity and function is helpful and healthy. Reclaiming your real estate starts with reframing your mindset.

REFRAMING QUESTIONS

1. When was the last time I needed an item like this?
2. When do I imagine myself using this item again?
3. How many of these items do I already have?
4. If given the opportunity to use this item in the future, would I choose this item or possibly a different but similar item?
5. Is this an item that could be easily replaced with little monetary reinvestment?
6. What space am I currently using to store this item now? Can this space be better utilized in another way?
7. What timeline do I give myself to use this item before I decide to let go of it?
8. Is there someone else that can use this item if I am not realistically going to use it in the near future?

* * * * *

R.E.C.L.A.I.M. Case Study

You Can Never Have Too Many

Our clients are a semi-retired married couple who are living in a three-bedroom home. They currently have two rooms that both have multiple uses. Their hope is to organize both rooms so that one can be used as a home office and the other used as a guest room when needed. Although both individuals are semi-retired, they both need personal work space that includes a filing system, desk space, and stored office supplies. The couple mentions that they rarely work at the same time; however, they prefer to have individual spaces to perform their work duties when needed. The current layout and functionality of these two rooms in their home is not meeting the clients' needs in their current life chapter.

Currently, the clients are using two large filing cabinets in separate rooms to store their work and personal paperwork. This system creates difficulty finding important documents when needed. The clients comment that as they have aged, their memory is not as sharp. They tend to set papers down and forget where they leave them. They need a centralized system that is easy to access and maintain, including a system for organizing and processing physical mail.

Before we started the **Reframe and R.E.C.L.A.I.M.** process, we asked a few questions to better understand our clients and their perspectives.

What have been the obstacles for you in assessing and evaluating the items you want to address today?

Wife: It's just a mess. It's just so unorganized. I thought we had it organized. Call us lazy. Because I get busy and go from one project to another, and then I just forget to put it back. We're guilty of not putting things back where they belong and we forget about it. Since we've been married. staying organized has been more challenging. I used to be more organized when I was younger but as we're getting older, I'm losing it.

How do you feel when you see this space today?
Wife: It makes you feel like there's so much chaos going on. We just don't have a lot of space.
Husband: It needs to be straightened up and we need to put things where they belong. I'm feeling aggravated.
Wife: I feel the same.

We will work together because we want to know what you love and what pieces you really want to look at daily because that's what is going to make it feel like home to you. It's the pieces that you really connect with, so we will work together to make it functional and aesthetically pleasing.

You two are making decisions. We are doing the work. And it is not us doing something with it; it is us doing what you want with the item. So if you want this desk here or you want these papers thrown away we're going to make sure everything goes where it needs to go. We want to make a system that works for you because you have tried systems before that have not worked.

As we start the R.E.C.L.A.I.M. process, we will go through the seven-step process below:

R – REFLECT on the current space.

How are these spaces currently being used?
Wife: They are not right now.
Husband: Right now, they're not particularly being used the way we want because we still have office stuff in the guest room and we still have guest stuff in here. Both of us have the tendency to spread stuff out.

What is your hope for the functionality of these spaces?
Husband: I would like the back room to be 100% strictly a guest room with the exception of the closet that has clothes my wife will never wear, but that's where she wants to have them. And I would like the front room to be a combination office, sitting room and guest room.
Wife: For me, I would like to be able to go to my particular work space and set it up like I like it. That's it. I want it to be functional but yet nice. Right now it's just cluttered.

How do you hope to feel when you see this space once the Reframe & Reclaim process is complete?
Wife: Happier, less stressed. Less stress on my mind.
Husband: Functional and not cluttered. I want things in their place. Structured.

What's given you the inspiration to start this today?
Husband: I was told we were gonna do it.
Wife: It makes me feel more comfortable that you're going to allow us to be a part of the process rather than having someone come in and say, "This needs to go here, this needs to go there."

E – EVALUATE each item and understand the true value each item has for you as you empty the space. Reimagine how this space functions. *How does each item fit into your aspirational space? Does each item match the feel and function you imagined for the space?*

The wife previously worked as a teacher and is very involved in her social club. She has purchased an abundance of office supplies for her past work and social activities, but now that she is retired from teaching, she no longer needs all of these supplies.

The excess office supplies that are no longer needed are consuming valuable real estate in her closet. The client hopes to use this storage space for office supplies and materials that she frequently uses now. Several times a month, she mails out greeting cards for her social club and needs easy access to these materials.

We begin by evaluating several boxes of office supplies found in the closet and in boxes scattered across the floor. The closet is currently organized with labeled shelves and baskets, but the supplies are overflowing and do not fit in their current designated places. The system that was once created has now become overwhelmed. For this client, it is important to realize how many of each item she has acquired so that she can declutter and allocate the appropriate amount of space to the office supplies and other items she chooses to keep.

We continuously find writing pens throughout the office space and boxes of clutter. There are easily hundreds of pens that have been collected, forgotten, and misplaced in their space. In the end of the Evaluation phase, the clients choose to keep only a handful of pens for each of their work stations, allowing them to discard and donate the overabundance of pens and free up valuable storage space in their home.

We discovered more than three rolls of postage stamps found in various bins, loose coins, forgotten gift cards, loose batteries, hundreds of greeting cards with envelopes, gift bags, address labels, business card templates, manilla folders, hanging file folders, printer paper, and ink cartridges for multiple printers. Surprisingly, many of the office supplies found were brand new and never used or opened. The clients were happily surprised to find the missing and newly found office supplies that were misplaced. Due to the lack of system maintenance, these supplies were purchased, misplaced, and repurchased throughout the years.

Wife: I don't think in my lifetime I'm ever going to need to buy paper again.

In the case of this couple, they do not know how many of each item they currently have in their possession, but by evaluating their space and physically seeing and touching each item, they are better able to realize all of the items they have in their home. As we sit and look at all of the office supplies in their space, we ask the clients about this process and insight they have about their habits.

Wife: I'm guilty of not remembering I have something and when I'm out, I think, "Oh, I need that," but I already have it.

Husband: One of the problems you can see already is that when we need something, instead of looking in here for it, we go buy it. We've got more file folders than we can ever use.

As we continue to evaluate the office supplies, the clients quickly learn to reflect, reframe, and be honest with themselves and their current lifestyle needs.

Through this process, the clients are realizing how much has accumulated over the years and what the clients realistically need for their lifestyle today.

Wife: Let's save those... No, never mind. I would never use them.

As we are reviewing and evaluating the office supplies with the wife, the husband is evaluating piles of paperwork on their various shelves and in the filing cabinets. He is able to declutter and discard many papers and old documents that are no longer needed. He also finds his misplaced passport among the piles of papers that he evaluates. We combine all of their personal and business files into one filing cabinet, discard a broken filing cabinet, and create a dedicated space for a shared printer and mail system.

As we continue to work through the R.E.C.L.A.I.M. process, we find a strategy that works well for this client. The wife chooses a box, tray, or bin where she wants to store each item for her reclaimed space. As we evaluate the supplies in the clients' space, she decides what items to keep according to what will fit into the allocated bins and storage areas. This strategy creates a physical boundary and limits the amount of items she can comfortably hold in the space. The client chooses to donate the excess items that do not fit into the physical space, allowing these unneeded items to be used by someone else. This process allows the client to keep an inventory of supplies but does not allow the space to be overwhelmed and disorganized.

After evaluating and decluttering the office supplies, the client chooses to keep only four containers of supplies. When we started this process, the closet was overflowing with office supplies. At the end of the Evaluate step, ten storage containers were emptied and are repurposed to create a new system to maintain organization and functionality of this space in their home. The client chooses to donate four large boxes of office supplies to a local organization that serves teachers.

Wife: I'm tickled to death a lot of the office supplies can be donated and it will help someone.

C – CLEAN the space. Empty and clean the space so that it feels like a fresh, clean slate.

How do you feel seeing this space empty versus how you felt with the space occupied with items?
Wife: Oh my goodness! Now I have closet space. I love it. We can even lower the shelves. I feel wonderful. We have space.
Husband: It feels better.
Wife: I can't thank you all enough for this.

It took us one hour and thirty-five minutes to do all this work, and you are only keeping four bins of supplies. We now have ten empty bins, we cleared off three storage shelves in the room. We can now use those shelves to display items. And we have four boxes to donate to a good cause.

L – LAYOUT and label the space before placing any items back into the space. Attempt to create a blueprint of how the space will look and feel. Measure and readjust the space to fit the space's new functionality, as well as any organizational materials that you may include to enhance the aesthetic and functionality.

What do you hope this space will be for you now that you have reflected and evaluated the items in this space and the space's function?
Wife: I want to be able to walk into the closet and look to my left and my right and find everything I need easily. I want it to be strictly for office use and to be organized and functional.

Once we empty and clean the closet space, we use Post-it notes to determine the layout of the office supplies that will be reorganized in the closet. The client states that she uses her greeting cards and stamps most frequently. These items are placed at eye level for easy access and visibility. We also keep similar items grouped together and place heavier items, including the paper shredder and reams of paper, on the floor and bottom shelves. Items that will be used less frequently are placed on higher shelves.

A – ASSEMBLE items back into the space and adjust as needed. Allow for trial and error as you reimagine the space's blueprint. This may be adjusting materials, changing where items are located, or reframing what items are truly intended for this new environment.

We begin by adjusting the shelves in the closet to accommodate the office supplies that will be stored. With all of the supplies removed from the closet, we are able to lower and appropriately space each shelf for easier access and increase functionality. This ensures that the space is used efficiently, maximizes functionality, and reduces wasted space. By labeling everything and allocating enough space for each item, we create a system that can be easily accessed and maintained. As long as the couple returns items to their labeled and allocated places, there will continue to be enough space for every item and enough extra space to restock items when inventory is low.

The client desires to have a stationary storage bin for her social club mailings. We are able to create a stationary station using two of the bins we emptied during the Evaluation step. We collect and categorize the greeting cards by type: Birthday, Get Well, Thank You, etc. This allows the client to easily find greeting cards and view the inventory she has before purchasing additional cards for her mailings. Now, the client can quickly access what she needs and spend her time writing a letter instead of searching for the cards.

We assemble two small working desks that fit comfortably in the newly created office space. Each desk has individually personalized supplies chosen by each client including pens, pencils, staplers, and staple removers. Now each client can easily access the office supplies used daily and maintain their personal work spaces.

Now that we have reassembled the office space, do you know where things are located? Do you feel comfortable with this office space?
Husband: Yes, everything is easily found with the exception of our files. It is our own doing from over twenty years of being married.

Now, the good news is, all of your files that you had in two separate filing cabinets are now in one filing cabinet. The next step is for you both to start organizing your papers. And now you can easily find the extra filing hanging files, tabs and a label maker to help you finalize your newly organized office space.

In the time allotted, we are able to create and organize an office space that will function for the clients. We did not evaluate the clients' personal files and documents due to the sensitivity of the information that may be found. The clients have discussed a plan and a system to conquer this last detailed step after working through the R.E.C.L.A.I.M. process with our support and guidance. The clients have learned strategies and learned actionable steps to continue this process on their own.

REFRAME & RECLAIM

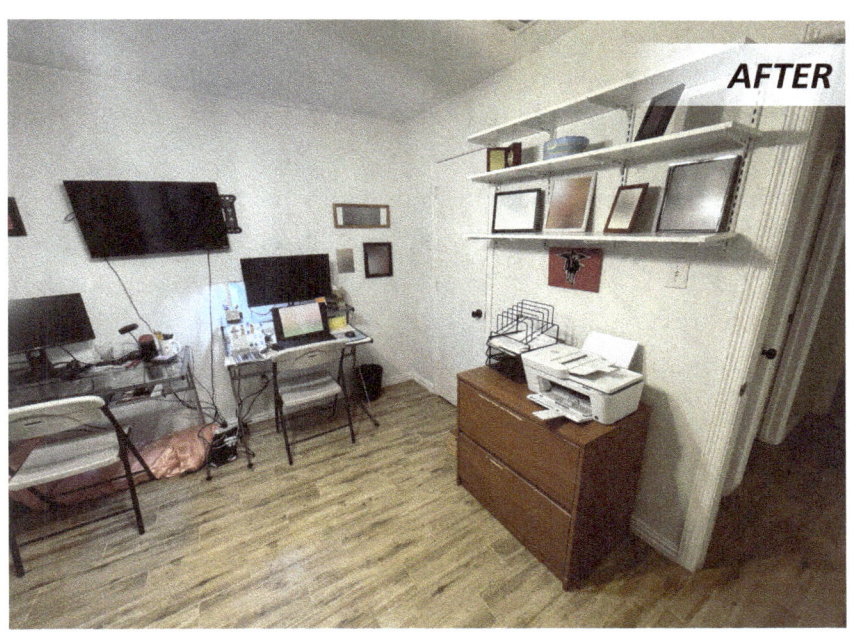

I – INSPECT the space once everything is reassembled. Step back and take inventory, viewing the aesthetic and functionality of the newly reimagined space. This is the final gut check.

Does this space now match the intention you imagined?
Husband: It would be how I would want it. If it is what I imagined or not, I don't know. But it's very much what we need. It is very workable and very doable.
Wife: And stress free.
Husband: Very pleasant to the eye.

M – MAINTAIN your space. Remember that this space will only stay as organized and aesthetically pleasing as you put effort and intentionality into it. Create a plan and a system to purposefully maintain this new space, recruiting any other people needed that utilize or enjoy this space. Accountability is key.

As we neared the end of the seven-step R.E.C.L.A.I.M. process with this client, we wanted to ensure that our clients have awareness and a plan of action to continue to maintain this beautiful space they have helped to create for their home.

What system will you put in place to keep this space as you see it today?
Wife: The two-second rule.
Husband: Well, the two and two. You look around the room for two seconds, and if something doesn't belong there and it takes less than two minutes, then you go put it up then.

What if it does take more than two minutes?
Husband: Well then, at that point, you have to plan the time to redo it, but ninety percent of the things you see can be taken care

of with the two and two rule. In addition to the "two and two" rule, we need to check the inventory before we go buy something.

What steps will you need to take to assure that this space will continue to function and feel like it does right now?

Wife: I'm going to have to ask myself, "Do I really need it? Or do I really want to keep this?"

Husband: And all our belongings will be passed down to the kids; so how many ballpoint pens do they want?

We also want to evaluate how our clients experienced the seven steps of R.E.C.L.A.I.M. We asked them the following questions:

How did you feel during the process?

Wife: I felt less stressed as I started seeing the visual clutter leaving the space. I was able to realize what this space could look like.

Was the R.E.C.L.A.I.M. process what you expected it to be?

Wife: No. I think it went better than I thought it was going to go. I thought it would be more stressful, and you made me feel comfortable. You helped me feel that it is okay to throw things away. And you kept us motivated. You reminded me to focus.

Husband: I didn't feel stressed.

Do you feel comfortable to continue this process now that you have experienced it today?

Wife: Yes. I can see what decluttering does. It makes you feel a lot better. It really does. Sometimes I think clutter can play on people's moods.

Husband: It is a team and an individual responsibility. If I walk through and I notice everything where it needs to be, or if it is out of place, all I need to do is pick up something and put it up.

What advice do you have for others that are unsure about starting or just beginning this process?

Wife: I think they need to do it. I really do. It lightened up my mood. It's a relief. Now, I know it is on us to keep it this way. Keep it organized. I think my work will be better because I know where everything is now. Before, I lost hope in getting things done. I'm here and there, and half the time I'm going in circles trying to find things.

Husband: She'll start doing something and forget. So there will be papers laying here and papers laying there.

Wife: We don't have to worry about that because it's all organized in this space now.

Any feedback you have for us as we have helped you facilitate this process?

Wife: Not really because you were so positive and encouraging, which helped tremendously. It wasn't, "Go do this! You need to do this!" It was a team effort. You encouraged us, "Let's keep going." You made me feel so comfortable. It really helped to have you doing all the physical work. I think we try to do it and we get tired of moving things around. We just can't thank you enough. I kept telling my husband, "I'm so excited they are going to come to R.E.C.L.A.I.M. us!"

FOLLOW-UP

A few months later, we contacted the clients to see if the new systems and separate workstations were still working for them. We also wanted to hear if the R.E.C.L.A.I.M. process motivated the clients to declutter the closet that was mentioned at our last interview. We asked the wife the following questions to get an update on their progress.

Now that you've lived with the system for a few months how does it feel?
Wife: It feels wonderful! I feel like I have control back. My husband still has some messy habits, but it is kept to his personal desk. I feel happy. I am happy.

Does it still work? Anything you would change?
Wife: It does still work. It is easy to work in. I would not change anything. The function is fantastic. I can walk into the closet and know exactly what I have. I'm not digging for items.

Do you have any regrets about letting go of any of your items?
Wife: Not a one.

How has this process helped you reframe your relationship with your things?
Wife: I seem like I have more control of my stuff since I know where it is. It is staying organized. I learned more organization skills.

Have you started to evaluate any other spaces in your home since your first R.E.C.L.A.I.M. process with us?
Wife: Yes, I was motivated to organize my closet. I used space saving hangers, and I love it. Now I can see the floor in my closet. In the past, I had two bars of hanging clothes, and could never see my shoes. Now I am getting ready to evaluate my guest room closet and have already gotten rid of some clothes. I have learned to let go.

* * * * *

For Your Personal R.E.C.L.A.I.M. Process

As you think about your own life, how are you spending your resources to store all of the items that "you can never have too many of" in your home? What are the time, mental, real estate, and financial tolls?

- How do you feel when you enter your home and see your items in your space? Is there a certain room or space of your home that causes more stress to you than others?
- Do the amount of items in your home cause stress or conflict between you and your family members?
- How much time have you spent looking for an item because you cannot find what you need? Do your important items easily get lost in the overabundance of things in your space?
- How many times have you purchased an item that you thought you had because you could not find it in your space?
- Have you purchased items in your home you have not used yet?
- Are you paying rent or mortgage to have space that is large enough to store all of your personal items?
- Are you spending money on a storage unit for items you are not currently using or rarely use? Will you use these items in the next six months or the next year?

These questions are a great start to reflect about your personal real estate and realize how your space feels for you and your family. Is your space functioning or dysfunctioning? Creating expectations and boundaries for yourself and your space can help you to determine how to begin the R.E.C.L.A.I.M. process for your real estate. How do you evaluate if you will or will not keep an item? Below are some strategies on how to start this process.

ONE IN AND ONE OUT

It is impossible to keep a space organized and a system working if you exceed the space you have previously allocated or if there is nowhere to place the items after you are finished using them. The "one in and one out" rule sets physical boundaries to maintain a space's integrity and functionality by limiting how many items can be stored or displayed in the identified space. If a new item is purchased, a current item in this space must be discarded or donated. For example, limit board games to two shelves in a closet. If another board game is purchased and does not fit on the allotted space, choose one board game to discard or donate to a local charity. This is a great strategy to use in order to maintain the spaces you have decluttered and ensure you do not consume more items than the space can accommodate. This strategy also forces a person to intentionally purchase new items rather than impulse buying.

20/20 RULE

A popular decluttering strategy introduced by The Minimalists, Joshua Fields Millburn and Ryan Nicodemus, is the 20/20 rule. This rule focuses on time and money parameters to evaluate items in your home. Can you replace this item by spending $20 or less and within twenty minutes or less? If an item can be easily replaced, letting go of this item may be a simple solution for spaces that are overwhelmed with stuff. This rule can be adjusted to any numbers that you feel comfortable with. If you are more comfortable and confident you will not need an item going forward, you can change the rule to $50 or less and thirty minutes or less. If the item you are needing to replace is not easily purchased, the timeline can be altered to best fit you and your lifestyle. This decluttering strategy can help you kickstart your journey to reclaim your real estate and reduce the urge to have more than you need.

TWO AND TWO RULE

The Two And Two Rule was referenced by the clients previously in this chapter. Starting in one room in your home, look around for two seconds for items that are not in their proper spaces. If you estimate that it will take you less than two minutes to pick up an item and place it in its proper home, take the time now to return the item to its proper place. This strategy may be more challenging for some than others, especially when moving from room to room. Remembering to only focus on one room at a time will allow for more success. Not only is this strategy simple and easy to accomplish, it is something that you can practice throughout your day. Instead of spending hours decluttering your home in one session, you can create a habit of looking for items out of place and returning them to their appropriate spaces throughout your day. This daily habit can reduce the amount of mental stress and time spent cleaning and organizing your home. Practicing the Two And Two Rule can reduce the amount of time spent cleaning if this is done more frequently rather than choosing one day to clean all areas of your home at once.

THE BASKET METHOD

The basket method is an additional way to declutter items in each room of your home. Grab a basket when looking through a room. When you find an item out of place, add it to the basket. Once the basket is full, or all of the misplaced items have been collected, return the items in the basket to their rightful place. Once the basket is emptied and the items have found their proper home, you can move to the next room or take a break.

TIMELINE STRATEGY

Giving yourself a personal timeline to use an item is another helpful strategy to ensure you are utilizing the items in your space. Give yourself a realistic timeline for you to use, wear, or display an item in your real estate. For example, if you have a closet full of clothes, ensure that you are actually wearing all of the clothes you store in your closet by setting a timeline of six months or a year to wear each item at least once. If you have not worn an item hanging in your closet within that timeline, donate it or give it to a friend or family member who will wear it.

> If I have not used or worn this item it in _____ months, I will choose to let this item go to someone who will use it.

> If I have not used or displayed this seasonal item during the specified season, I will choose to let this item go to someone who will use it or display it.

HOME DECOR VERSUS HOME FUNCTIONALITY

Your home decoration should not limit or hinder your home's daily function. Assuring that everyone in the home is comfortable with the decoration and function of the home is important. Limiting special occasion decoration to specific areas of the home that are not used daily can be a helpful solution. For example, you may limit Halloween decorations to the children's playroom or an entryway and front yard. For the Christmas season, you can enjoy the festivities of the season with holiday cheer, but be mindful to not overwhelm your everyday kitchen and eating areas with tinsel and lights.

If you live with others, be sure to include them in your decorating and storage solutions so that others are involved in helping to maintain the agreed upon system and keep each other accountable. This is an excellent time to discuss strategies to compromise and meet each other's daily needs. Reflecting and evaluating your personal values and boundaries will help you to decide what is most important for you and your family goals. Identifying and aligning the goals for your home's functionality can create peace and harmony for your space and in your family relationships.

Ultimately, this is *your* life journey. There are no wrong answers, and there are multiple solutions and compromises you can make in aligning your goals with your current chapter of life. What strategies can you adopt to reclaim your space to make room for what is really important to you or your family values?

If "You can never have too many" strikes a chord with you and you are ready to take action in your space, reference the Tips for Your Personal Reframe & R.E.C.L.A.I.M. Process at the end of our book.

CHAPTER 3

I MAY USE IT ONE DAY

*"Remember: Your Home is not a store.
You don't need to save everything 'just in case.'"*
– Anonymous

Jennifer

Being a child that grew up with landlines, DSL, and power A/C adaptors, I know the headache of misplacing a cord. There was a solid six months I could not play my Rap Master keyboard because the power cord had been misplaced. It was battery operated but the 5AA batteries required to power it would only last a couple weeks before needing to be replaced again. Therefore, holding onto miscellaneous power cords and wires was necessary for electronic survival.

During my young life, we did not simply have a USB adapter to plug into a wall. Every electronic item and appliance had its own cord, and if you lost it, you would have to trek down to your local

Radio Shack store in search for the exact cord or wire you needed. So if I came across a random power cord, telephone cable, or input jack, I always kept it and stored it away. The cords and wires stayed stored away in a tangled and knotted electronic purgatory because I might possibly use them one day.

In most homes, a junk drawer can be found, but I know several households that have the infamous junk cable box. Twenty years later, I continue to hold onto a box of random cords and wires even though I have no idea which electronic item they belong to or if the cord even works. These possibly useless cords and wires continue taking up valuable real estate in my home for fear that one day I will find the elusive electronic item it belongs to. But the truth is, if I ever need that random cord, will I know where to find it? Or with access to products being so readily available online will I just buy a new one?

There are two utilitarian excuses: "I can never have too many" and "I may use it one day." Of the two excuses, "I may use it one day" is the excuse that keeps me holding onto the most clutter. There are several bags for me to unpack in this chapter, and they are all full of anxiety and guilt. I feel anxious that I might need this random item one day. However, if I do choose to discard this infrequently used thing, I will feel guilty that I discarded it and now must purchase another to replace it. The single junk drawer in most homes does not compare to the junk bins I store in my garage. While my garage is not filled with scraps of wood and knick-knacks like my grandfather's basement, to an outsider, many would perceive this valuable real estate as being wasted.

One day, Courtney and I were discussing organization and what types of containers I liked to use for various projects. I proudly shared about the neatly arranged storage shelves in my garage that I utilize to house my extra empty storage containers. I keep these because I "might use them one day" for the reorganization of my home if needed. Surprisingly to me, she was not impressed with my amazing home organizational storage area. Instead, she made the comment, "Wait, you have storage for your storage bins?"

Of course, I do. I had a system, and it made perfect sense to me. I had my favorite bins that I believed would be the solution to an imaginary future organization problem. Therefore, I justified the real estate that the empty storage bins consumed. Large bins that once held holiday decorations, medium-sized baskets that I used to organize my kids' toys, smaller containers that I have used for organizing shelves, magazine holders, drawer dividers, rolling carts, and hanging closet organizers were now warehoused in the back corner of my garage as my own personal storefront. I love organizing, so for me, this was simply being resourceful, right?

I know rationally that I did not want to store additional items in the garage. I was on a mission to organize and purge more. However, the habitual side of me still felt the pull to keep the bins in case I might need them one day. How could I be wasteful and discard these useful containers? I may find a new life and purpose for them. So there the bins sat empty, taking up valuable space in my garage shelving unit.

Storing the "one day" items is also seen on a daily basis at the top shelf of my closet. This is where the aspirational portion of my closet lives. My weight has fluctuated since my senior year of high school, so keeping clothes for my future self is a one-to-two-bin situation on my top shelf at all times. My mindset for the past twenty plus years has been that if this pair of jeans fit perfectly and made me feel confident ten years ago, then they were worth storing for the future me. I was delusional to think that I would feel the same level of confidence in them as I did the first time I wore them.

Fast forward to 2016, when I was pregnant with my first child. I went through a deep nesting period and donated all of my "single lady" clothes including my six-inch red heels and short clubbing outfits that I knew I would never wear again. Clubbing was not what life had in store for me going forward. I was secure closing that chapter of my life, but I held onto the everyday and business attire from my twenties, whether the clothes fit me today or fifteen years prior. For some reason, I believed that by re-wearing these beloved clothes that held great memories, I would feel the same way as I did the first time I wore them.

But nine out of ten times, once I could fit back into the item of clothing, I never felt the same. I could not recreate those moments because even after only a couple years I was a different person with different intentions and a different lifestyle. Like my storage bins, I constantly found my new "favorite" piece of clothing, and the clothes I swore I would wear again stayed in the back of my closet. Even when I had the opportunity to wear a piece I had saved for years, It remained hanging because I found my new favorite piece I preferred to wear. So again, these clothes sat in a closet taking up valuable real estate. Do you see a pattern?

Another issue is the elastic items I was storing became stretched out and lost their elasticity. Even in a temperature controlled room, the elastic wears out and is no longer usable after so long. In hindsight, it would have been better to donate the items to someone who would wear the item while it was still useful, instead of the item wasting away in a closet, only to end up in a landfill. But just like fashion changes and you acquire new favorites, other parts of our lives will continue to evolve with new wants and needs.

If you have not figured it out by now, my core value of being resourceful and not wasteful is very strong for me. So I justify keeping these items because of the guilt of buying the item, spending my hard earned money, and then not using it, which would be the epitome of wastefulness. For me, it is the equivalent of throwing my money out the door.

But the truth is the money is already spent. I have to reframe my thinking and change my thoughts from, "I have wasted money," to "This is the amount of money it has cost me to learn this valuable lesson," so that I will not be wasteful going forward.

REFRAME

> *"All men know the utility of useful things; but they do not know the utility of futility."*
> – Zhuangzi

Courtney

Utility and function of objects help make life easier. Whether it is a screwdriver to tighten a loose screw on a cabinet door or a collection of loose screws I have found, objects come in handy and can create solutions when needed. Keeping objects "just in case" can create a quick solution and save possible time searching for and purchasing something needed in the future. However, having a "just in case" item for multiple situations can overwhelm and create clutter and chaos for some, especially when the probability of needing said object is slim to none.

Please do not misinterpret that we believe you do not need any items "just in case." It is helpful and resourceful to keep items that you will actually use. It is only when we overestimate the usefulness of over-collected items that they begin to overtake and over clutter your real estate. This clutter can interfere with the function of your home and the need to now find storage space for the items that you may possibly need someday.

For instance, if you have a junk drawer filled with all of your "just in case" items, not only are you losing a valuable drawer space for useful items that you may use more often, but you may also forget the item is even there. Worse yet, you may forget that you have the possibly useful item and not be able to use it because it is lost in all of the stuff we choose to keep and store. The junk drawer, at times, can grow into the junk closet or junk room. According to ClearVoice Research, one in seven Americans have a room in their home they cannot use because it is filled with things they rarely use.

In the long run, the "I may use it one day" items can cause more harm than good. The money you have chosen to invest in this resourceful item, the time it takes to search for and locate the "keep just in case" items and the space utilized or wasted to store these items can add up quickly. What was once a great idea to keep items that can possibly be of good use one day can become a chaotic storage of many bits and thingamabobs. Junk drawer purgatory is an unfortunate place for so many "what if I may use these items" all over the world.

To reframe this mindset, it can be helpful to evaluate the likelihood that you will use this item in the future. What is the likelihood that I will use eighteen strings of yarn if I am not a knitter or crafter? Or how likely is it that I will realistically use the Allen wrench provided in the furniture kit to assemble the kids' new bunk beds? Is it valuable enough to keep nine Allen wrenches, all the same size, so that I will have these items if needed one day? Or is investing in an Allen wrench kit with various sizes sufficient for me so that I can discard the unused furniture assembly kits? How likely am I to realistically find time and projects to use these items? And how much space am I willing to give up to store these things in my home, office, or storage space?

For some people, this mindset and practice is something that was role modeled for them by their parents, grandparents, or other family members. Some have grown up with the mindset to not be wasteful and prioritizing resourcefulness and reusing or repurposing items. This is a noble philosophy and perspective if you can use the items that you are keeping. The justification of keeping and collecting an item needs to be based on the realistic possibility of actually using the item. Otherwise, we are keeping and collecting things that ultimately become clutter. Function and facility are an important focus for a healthy and well-established home environment.

If you are a person that despises wastefulness, there are many organizations where you can donate unused items. Please see the resource pages "Resources for Selling Your Unwanted Items" and "Resources for Donating Your Unwanted Items" at the back of this book. For people who value resourcefulness, responsible consumerism, and conservation, this is a win-win! Your home becomes more functional and comfortable, and you are assisting organizations and causes to give back, recycle, and conserve resources so that the items can fulfill their purpose. Being a part of the movement to reuse items to meet community needs is not only philanthropic, it is also generous and responsible. Not only can your personal real estate be reclaimed, your mental peace of mind as well as your community involvement can be instilled again.

Reframing the possibility of usefulness an object can give you is vital in helping you filter through and declutter your real estate. The questions below can be helpful tools in beginning your reframe process and identifying items in your space that are most useful and realistically going to be functional for your space.

REFRAMING QUESTIONS

1. When was the last time I needed an item like this?
2. When do I imagine myself using this item again?
3. How many of these items do I already have?
4. If given the opportunity to use this item in the future, would I choose this item or a possibly different but similar item?
5. Is this an item that could be easily replaced with little monetary reinvestment?
6. What space am I currently using to store this item now? Can this space be better utilized in another way?
7. What timeline do I give myself to use this item before I decide to let go of it?
8. Is there someone else that can use this item if I am not realistically going to use it in the near future?

Once you begin to reframe the realistic usefulness and realistic possibility of actually using your items in your possession, you may begin to see patterns emerge. The felt responsibility and resourcefulness of keeping "just in case" things may have brought you excitement, joy, and feelings of security and safety. However, over time, this continued habit of keeping things "because I may need it one day" can create a heavy weight and overwhelm you. The sheer amount of objects that are kept because it may be needed one day can almost overpower a space and crush a person's spirit once you begin to see how much you have collected over time.

If this is you, start small. Begin with one drawer or one box. Starting somewhere is where the process begins and where progress creates momentum. You may be surprised how quickly you can work through small spaces, and over time, these small spaces really do add up. The weight and pressure of holding onto these items begins to lift as you find your spirits lift in relief and responsibility for beginning to reclaim your space and functionality for your home and your realistic needs today.

* * * * *

R.E.C.L.A.I.M. Case Study

I May Use It One Day

The client in this chapter is a young, creative woman who has moved out of her mother's home a year prior. When moving out of her childhood home, she decided to leave behind items that she did not need immediately. Her mother has been gracious to let her continue to store her personal items that did not fit in the small apartment she rents with a roommate. However, after nine months of living independently, her mother has requested that the client reduce the amount of stored items in her home and begin moving her personal belongings to her apartment.

In the family room of her mother's house, five bins, two large rolling drawer carts and several bags of miscellaneous art supplies are being stored in a three-foot by five-foot section against a wall. Although the art supplies are stored in one section of the room, the pile is immediately seen as you walk into the room. The overflow of items being stored encroaches into the walkway leading to the guest room.

Now that our client is living independently, she has learned more about herself and is considering more life changes in the near future. She tells us she is ready to close one chapter of her past life – childhood – and start another with our help. As a young and creative person, she has always been drawn to expressing herself through art. The art supplies are reflective of her passion and investment in her personal art journey. The art mediums range from beads, stamps, markers, paints, yarns, and fabrics.

As we begin our **Reframe and R.E.C.L.A.I.M.** process, we asked a few questions to better understand our client and her perspectives.

What have been the obstacles for you in assessing and evaluating the items you want to address today?

Just the sheer amount of stuff. When you're an artist, you tend to gravitate toward art supplies you don't necessarily need, but you're like, "Oh, I'll use that one day. I want to try out this new thing." And then they just pile up after a while and it's like, "Did I ever use that? Am I going to use it?"

How long have you been accumulating the items we will be reviewing today?

Years. Probably about a decade. Because some are older art supplies I had from school and others I've acquired as I've grown as an artist.

How do you feel when you see this space today?

A little chaotic. Unsure. There's a lot of stuff, but I think that's the nature of artists in general – everything is a little on the chaotic side.

Is there anything about this process that you think may be uncomfortable for you?
The whole mindset of just being like, am I going to use that in the future? I think that's going to be the biggest struggle. Which is saying a lot for me because I've been going through some stuff with my mother recently and it's actually been pretty easy for me to make decisions.

As we start the R.E.C.L.A.I.M. process, we will go through the seven-step process below:

R – REFLECT on the current space.

How is this space currently being used?
Not well. It is being used as storage.

How do you hope to feel when you see this space once the Reframe & Reclaim process is complete?
Relieved. I guess I feel like a weight, regardless how heavy it is, will have been lifted. I want the space to feel creative and flowy and organized.

What are your hopes in going through the editing and decluttering process?
To get rid of the art supplies I no longer need or use and to make space. It's literally just sitting here.

What's given you the inspiration to start this today?
I've changed a lot in the past couple years. I'm starting to realize a lot of things about not only myself and my brain is starting to shift. I guess you could say…evolving

So maybe what you have needs to evolve as well.
Exactly. I've grown a lot in the past couple years. Especially with my self-confidence and my self-esteem.

When you're confident in yourself, you can make more confident decisions. And I don't need stuff to help me feel confident because I'm confident in who I am and the stuff is just extra. Sometimes when we don't feel so confident in ourselves, having things gives us some validation.
Yeah, that makes a lot of sense. Again, I've been struggling with a lot of things not only with myself but relationships and that makes a lot of sense.

Our hope is that we are here to help you. Remember this is a process where you make decisions. We're just here to help you along the way so it's not just you all on your own.

E – EVALUATE each item and understand the true value each item has for you as you empty the space. Reimagine how this space functions. *How does each item fit into your aspirational space? Does each item match the feel and function you imagined for the space?*

Understanding that there are hundreds, if not, thousands of items to evaluate. Our hope is to reduce the feelings of overwhelm and allow the client to focus on one small portion at a time. Currently, bins are filled with multiple art mediums that have been purchased and gifted to the client over the last decade.

During this step of the R.E.C.L.A.I.M. process, we create different boxes and label each "Keep," "Donate," "Sell," and "Discard." We begin sorting through the art supplies one bin or box at a time.

As the client looks through all of her art supplies, she is able to quickly decide which items will be placed in which newly labeled box. Once each newly labeled box is filled, we move it out of the room to create more space to sort and evaluate supplies.

You told us that you have started some of the decluttering process with your Mom before we arrived today. So how's that been for you?
It's actually been really good. Like you said, I'm not living here anymore so it's been a little different. What happens is she sends me pictures. We text each other. We've also tried Facetime, but with the pictures it's really nice for me because I get overwhelmed very easily. So I think starting with the pictures it wasn't as easy for me to get overwhelmed. I wasn't seeing everything all at once. It was one item or a group of items.

There's a lot of overwhelm that comes with so much stuff. But it sounds like all of the things you have had have met a need or a want in your life. But you're evolving. Especially in this last year, you're not living here anymore. Maybe you don't need some of this stuff anymore. It has fulfilled a purpose.
Yeah, I noticed when we started doing this that my thought process has really evolved as well. Because normally, I would have kept everything or almost everything. But now my thought process, is a lot different. I noticed I've been like, "Oh, I know I want to keep this, but I know I'm not going to use it." Or, "This is something I really liked a few years ago. Do I really need it anymore?"

Through the evaluation process, we continue to learn more about this client. Over the many years of being an artist and experimenting with various art mediums, she shares how her personal art style has evolved as she has evolved as an artist.

Client: I don't really use traditional mediums as much anymore. I do a lot more digital art now because it's a lot more convenient. Digital art is so much easier because you have all your tools in one spot and it takes up less space. It's also really nice because if you make a mistake you can also just go back and fix it.

So we are hearing that you are not only growing as an artist, but you are also growing and realizing what materials you need and enjoy as an artist. So the mediums we may go through today may have been wonderful in a past chapter. Our hope is if we do find something that is still good and usable, we find someone that can use it. Because there are other artists that may love using these mediums. How long do you think these art materials have been sitting in this space?
Years, five, maybe more. It's probably been a year or two that they have not been used.

What were your hopes when you acquired these items?
To try something new. Use my creativity.

In the past when you would try something new, would you typically purchase a lot of things for this hobby or would you just dabble a little bit?
It depended on the hobby. This is something I've struggled with a lot because of my ADHD – I tend to try new mediums and I think you're going to love doing it and then I try it for a week and I'm done. And you have all these supplies left over. In high school and growing up, I really wanted to try things out but my attention span didn't last; so, it just wouldn't work out. With crocheting, I bought a bunch of yarn and a bunch of stuff I didn't necessarily need because I didn't know where to start. I tried it and it was very difficult and complicated. I couldn't figure it out, I thought, "Well, there's another hobby out the door." But with other things, it may have just been, "Oh, I'll just get this little kit or this item."

Creative people are willing and open to try a lot of things, but that is when we sometimes create spaces like this. But if the space is not helpful for you, we want to help you create a space that is functional for your creativity.

What are your hopes for these items now?
I'm hoping to donate and find someone else that will get use of them or if it's not usable, like dried up paint, throwing it out.

The client evaluated thousands of items during this step. It was an exhaustive step but rewarding. She was able to reduce the amount of art supplies that she hoped to keep and utilize to only one large bin. She sorted and decided to donate six boxes of usable art supplies to a local charity, discard five bags of trash containing old and unusable art supplies, and store one bin of higher quality goods to sell. Two tower rolling carts, and three bins were completely emptied and now able to be reclaimed and used in a different way if needed. Once the evaluation process was complete, the space that was previously occupied with stored art supplies was empty.

C – CLEAN the space. Empty and clean the space so that it feels like a fresh, clean slate.

How do you feel seeing this space empty versus how you felt with the space occupied with items?
I definitely feel that the weight is being lifted. I feel accomplished, relieved, and tired. I have just been sitting here looking at art supplies and making decisions. One of the last bins was the itty bitty stuff I never went through because it just gets so overwhelming. I realize how tired our brains can get when making decisions.

With this space now clean, this area can now be reframed and reclaimed for a different use other than a storage space. Because the space that was evaluatec today was not the client's current residence, we asked her mother to join us to discuss how she may want to reclaim and utilize this newly decluttered space in her home.

L – LAYOUT and label the space before placing any items back into the space. Attempt to create a blueprint of how the space will look and feel. Measure and readjust the space to fit the space's new functionality, as well as any organizational materials that you may include to enhance the aesthetic and functionality.

The process for this client was to reclaim what items were most useful for her current chapter in life. This case study was focused on removing items from the client's childhood home. Because of this, the layout step of the R.E.C.L.A.I.M. process will be decided by her mother, to reclaim the space for a new function and design. We sat with both the client and her mother to discuss the process and hopes for the current area in this home.

What do you hope this space will be for you now that you have reflected and evaluated the items in this space and the space's function?
Client's Mother: I'm not sure yet, but it's nice to see an open wall and a plug that can now be reached.

What do you hope this space will be for your mom now that you have reflected and evaluated the items in this space?
Client: I hope it will be a positive space that she can do something with.

How do you feel in this space knowing your daughter put all this hard work into this?
Client's Mother: It's fabulous! The room is more navigable now and my daughter kept what is most important to her. I am very impressed. I am very proud of my daughter for taking the time to do this. I appreciate you ladies helping with it because it is overwhelming if you tackle it all by yourself.

A – ASSEMBLE items back into the space and adjust as needed. Allow for trial and error as you reimagine the space's blueprint. This may be adjusting materials, changing where items are located, or reframing what items are truly intended for this new environment.

We realize this is a personal process for everyone and modifications may be needed. Our hope is for this client to find motivation, inspiration, and feelings of accomplishment in the R.E.C.L.A.I.M. process to be able to continue with other items in her childhood home.

Because the client's mother has not yet reimagined how to utilize this newly emptied space for her own personal function, we chose not to assemble this area at this time. In this case study, it is a win-win for both the client and her mother. Both are reframing and reclaiming on their own accord. The client is reframing her identity and reclaiming the art supplies that will best be utilized in her life today. The client's mother is embarking on a journey to reframe her identity and reclaim the functionality of her home without children.

I – INSPECT the space once everything is reassembled. Step back and take inventory, viewing the aesthetic and functionality of the newly reimagined space. This is the final gut check.

Because this family room had become a storage area, there are other items from the client's childhood that need to be evaluated before this process can be fully executed. Our hope is that this client will find inspiration and motivation to continue the R.E.C.L.A.I.M. process to reframe, evaluate, and reclaim the possessions being stored in her mother's home. Once this process is complete, the mother will be able to reframe, reimagine, and reclaim the space that is currently being used as a storage facility. She will be able to find her own inspiration and intention for a newly functional space that meets her lifestyle wants and needs.

M – MAINTAIN your space. Remember that this space will only stay as organized and aesthetically pleasing as you put effort and intentionality into it. Create a plan and a system to purposefully maintain this new space, recruiting any other people needed that utilize or enjoy this space. Accountability is key.

Through the Reframe and R.E.C.L.A.I.M. process, this client has realized that her previous mindset and past habits have created impulsive purchases of art supplies and mediums that have gone unused. Although her original intent was to "use it one day," the reality is that she continued to purchase and collect art supplies that were never utilized. In addition to these items not being used as intended, the client has also realized her Investments of time, money spent, and space used to store and collect these items for over a decade. The art supplies continued to collect as she changed and grew as an artist. Now, she has a clearer identity as an artist and is ready to share her unwanted art supplies with other artists.

As we neared the end of the seven-step R.E.C.L.A.I.M. process with this client, we wanted to ensure that our client had awareness and a plan of action to continue to maintain this beautiful space she had helped to create for her home.

What system will you put in place to keep this space as you see it today?
Reminding myself quality over quantity.

As an artist and creative person, how do you feel taking out the items you are no longer using? How is that going to affect your art and your creative process moving forward?
I think it's going to help because, while I like traditional mediums, I've been doing more artwork digitally. So am I really going to use this stuff since I've been sticking to the digital side? It's nice to have some things. I just don't need as much as I used to.

You've paired it down to your favorites. Your Quality over Quantity. We even heard you say that a couple times when you were going through your things. You said, "There's more value in this because there's more variation of colors," or "That was something that I used then but I don't use it now." What would that look like in your future when you're thinking of new art materials? What steps will you need to take to assure that this space will continue to function and feel like it does right now?
For example, if I am walking through a craft store and I see a new item like new pens and I think, "Oh, I haven't tried these out yet. Let me take a look at them. Oh. Wait! I've used something like this before. I don't need this right now," – that sort of thing.

So you have reframed your mindset from "I might use it one day" to "I do not need this right now." Do you feel like you can continue to reframe this mindset?
Yeah, I do.

With the client's renewed mindset, we hope she continues the hard work she has accomplished during this R.E.C.L.A.I.M. process. As she has reframed her mindset surrounding her art supplies, she realizes she has grown and will continue to evolve as an artist. However, she has gained confidence in her decision-making and self-accountability. This will serve her as she continues to grow as an artist.

We discuss what her ideas and perspectives are now that we are finishing the last step of the R.E.C.L.A.I.M. process.

How did you feel during the process?
Again, I could feel the weight lifting. I could feel like each bin we went through I could feel another weight being lifted. I could feel the energy of the room changing.

The energy feels different here. This room functioned as a storage space, and now it can be used for something new.

Was the R.E.C.L.A.I.M. process what you expected it to be?
Yes and no. I knew what to expect from the physical standpoint, the process of going through the stuff, but I was expecting it to be a lot harder. I know I am pretty quick at going through stuff, but I thought I was going to be clinging onto things more and not wanting to give things up. With you being here and having accountability, I felt more confident in letting things go.

I remember you said you thought it would take days.
Oh, yeah. Especially for everything in the house, it would take days. For the bins we did today it did not take as long as I thought it would. I thought it would take at least a day, like eight hours – but it took half the time.

What do you think it was about having us here that changed this mindset for you?
I think because you are here my brain just knew what my priorities are. What do I really want? And I guess having someone there just grounds you and does not allow you to second guess. Go with your gut instinct, go or keep. Of course, there were a couple times where I was unsure… "Do I keep it?" – but then you get back in your head and make a decision.

So having us here helped you stay grounded – focused?
Yeah, but it was also good because I never felt like I was being pushed. It goes back to what I was feeling in the beginning. It can get overwhelming and feel like, "You have to do this. You have to get this done." I never once felt like I was being judged for keeping or getting rid of an item.

Do you feel comfortable to continue this process now that you have experienced it today?
Yeah. It's still always going to feel a little overwhelming, but I don't think I will feel AS overwhelmed. Especially, since we went through a big chunk of stuff. Yeah there's still a bunch of stuff to go through, but I think, you know, the fact that we did it and we took the time and we can see it is manageable. You can get a big amount done in a short period of time. So, yeah, I think that makes it less overwhelming.

What space do you hope to evaluate next?
Maybe my bedroom or desk.

What advice do you have for others that are unsure about starting or just beginning this process?
I think the best advice is don't get too much into your own head. Don't let your insecurities get in your way. Again, this is one of the things I struggle with. I get overwhelmed easily. People tell me to do something and then it makes me not want to do it more because I get overwhelmed. When I see something I'm like, "I know I need to go through it, but I just don't have the mental capacity to do it." I think a big thing is don't second guess yourself. Don't underestimate yourself. You can do it. It's going to take time, and it's a lot of work. But you can do it, and in the end it's going to be better for you.

FOLLOW-UP

We contacted this client and her mother after we completed the R.E.C.L.A.I.M. process to check in and hear more about their experience. During the process, the client mentioned how she was attempting to reframe her mindset to think about quality over quantity rather than impulse buying. We wanted to see if the new mindset was taking hold or if she was slipping back into old habits and patterns. We asked the following questions below to find out.

Now that you've lived with the system for a few months how does it feel?
Client: Great. Relieved. It's nice being able to look in that room and corner where everything was and know that it is not being taken over anymore by stuff that is not being used. The space has a purpose now.

Client's Mother: Well it still feels fabulous because that room is not clogged with bins and boxes and everything else. I don't have the room totally organized because my daughter still has other things stored in this room, but the visual clutter is greatly reduced. A plus is when she comes back, she will be able to find her art supplies because they are centralized and not scattered all over the house.

Do you have any regrets about letting go of any of your items?
Client: Not doing this sooner. It was stuff that was just sitting there.

How has this process helped you reframe your relationship with your things?
Client: It helped me realize which art supplies I really don't need. Now, I realize what I am passionate about and more conscious of which art supplies I am going to use. I've come to realize I don't need to try every art medium.

Have you started to evaluate any other spaces in your home since your first R.E.C.L.A.I.M. process with us?
Client: Yes. After we were done with the art supplies, I was motivated and jumped right into decluttering my desk. Next, I want to work on my clothes and all my plushies.

* * * *

For Your Personal R.E.C.L.A.I.M. Process

Letting go of useful items is challenging for so many people. This is why we must evaluate our own personal needs and current life chapter to decide how useful each item is for us. The wonderful piece of this chapter is that the client was able to repurpose and re-home many useful items to others so that they can use them. The art supplies were sitting in boxes, collecting dust and some of the materials expired and were no longer useful. However, the materials she no longer needs or uses can be given life again.

Thinking about your own individual space and items you keep, reframing your personal need for each item and its usefulness can be freeing. Finding space to store items and attempting to find items once they have been stored away can be overwhelming. However, when you begin to reevaluate your need for each item, clearing your space and decluttering your home can be a weight lifted. Not only does your space begin to function better for you, you also begin to feel better. We can begin to think more clearly and feel more content when our space is also tidy and organized.

Here are some strategies to apply as you begin your personal R.E.C.L.A.I.M. process.

- Find empty containers you can use to evaluate and sort your items.
- Label each container: "Donate," "Sell," "Keep," and "Trash."
- Only keep the needed items that fit into the space you have allocated.
- Ask yourself the following reframing questions as you evaluate each item in your space:

1. When was the last time I needed an item like this?
2. When do I imagine myself using this item again?
3. How many of these items do I already have?
4. If given the opportunity to use this item in the future, would I choose this item or a possible different but similar item?
5. Is this an item that could be easily replaced with little monetary reinvestment?
6. What space am I currently using to store this item now? Can this space be better utilized in another way?
7. What realistic timeline do I give myself to use this item before I decide to let go of it? If you have not used the item in six months or at most in one year, for a seasonal item, is this an item that you have outgrown?
8. Is there someone else that can use this item if I am not realistically going to use it in the near future? Will this item lose its usefulness by the time I am able to use it?

Start small when you begin this process. Find a drawer or a cabinet. Take out items that you have not seen or do not remember storing away. Identify people or organizations that could make good use out of each of these unused and sometimes forgotten items. Work your way slowly through your spaces and start to feel the transformation of your space and yourself.

If you do not know where to start in selling or donating your discarded items, please refer to the resource pages at the end of this book: "Resources for Selling Your Unwanted Items" and "Resources for Donating Your Unwanted Items."

If "I may use it one day" strikes a chord with you and you are ready to take action in your space, reference the Tips for Your Personal Reframe & R.E.C.L.A.I.M. Process at the end of our book.

CHAPTER 4

IT'S SUCH A GOOD DEAL

*"Some people brag about how expensive their clothes are.
I brag about how cheap mine are."*
– Anonymous

Jennifer

Finding a good deal is one of the main excuses I use to justify my purchasing habits. Growing up, my family enjoyed the hunt for a good bargain (in a Bostonian accent). If we could buy a shirt for $2.00, it was a great deal. But, if it was a great deal purchasing one item, then buying five made it an amazing deal. I learned this purchasing habit at a young age and continue to feel pride and excitement when I find a deal today.

As a child, we visited family every summer in Maine, and completed our back to school clothes shopping before returning to Texas to start the new school year. Being from Texas, we shopped in the summer clearance aisles of clothing. As the weather in the Northeast turned cooler, the Texas heat remained constant, allowing us to wear summer attire almost year round. My closet was filled with bargain clothes, but in reality I was never going to wear all of them. By the time laundry was done and my favorite outfits were available to wear again, the bargain backups were lost in the depths of my closet of clothing despair. All of the money we saved in purchasing these great deals honestly became a loss of money when I consider how little I wore each piece of clothing.

Soon, all the extra clothing became visual clutter and increased my stress each time I looked in my closet. My closet was so full that, "I had nothing to wear," became my usual complaint. All in all, the amazing deals we purchased in the Northeast traveled halfway across the country and ended up living in and cluttering my closet space. Looking back now, I realize that the satisfaction I felt in finding a good deal was overshadowed later by the mental stress of seeing my overpacked closet. Additionally, the financial wastefulness of not wearing the bargain items added monetary stress as I became an adult and practiced these purchasing habits.

For the past several years, one of my favorite parts of Christmas is wrapping gifts. I turn on holiday movies, create my wrapping station on the dining room table and wrap away. I use extra tags, ornaments, and ribbons to embellish my gifts to add a layer of beauty under my tree. This is one of my creative outlets. Every January, after the Christmas rush is complete, I go and purchase new coordinating wrapping paper and embellishments to store away and use for the next Christmas holiday. When markdowns are seventy-five to ninety percent off the original sales price, I cannot resist the amazing money saving deals. I justify these purchases because I know I will use these items to create more beautiful gifts under my tree.

Honestly, I do use the gift wrap, but I rarely ever use the entire roll in one year because I like to use five or six different coordinating wrapping paper patterns each year. Although I am purchasing new wrapping paper each year, I continually have leftovers from previous years. In fact, at this moment, I have forty-three rolls of wrapping paper and over seventy-five gift tags and wrapping embellishments stored in my gift wrap bins. Will I ever use all the paper and tags? No. Using all of the wrapping paper on the roll rarely happens in my life. So much so that I feel like I should win an award if I can achieve that goal. I feel the same about using the entire Chapstick tube without losing it or washing it in the laundry.

Why is it so hard to resist the urge to buy wrapping paper when it is marked down and I still have wrapping paper at home? I obviously do not need any more Christmas gift wrap, but you better believe that if it is a good deal, I will justify buying more.

I previously worked for a large craft supply retailer at the corporate level. There was a mock-up store in our offices to setup store displays for each season. Proposed samples were sent to this mock-up store so that teams could categorize and create the store merchandise layout fcr all the stores in the company. Once the items were selected, orders were placed for these items, marketing photos were taken in preparation for advertising, and merchandise layouts were created for stores to recreate the map of the store. Then, all items went to the much-anticipated sample sale.

Several times a year, these items were deeply discounted and available for purchase by employees. These employee-only sample sales allowed me to shop the countless boxes of samples that were going to be discarded. For a mere $10.00, I stuffed a grocery-size bag with all the goodies I desired. With these great prices, the sample sales quickly turned into a Black Friday mad dash. Employees showed up hours before the sample sale started to get a prime spot in line and have the best opportunity to find the hidden treasures they did not know they wanted or needed.

Needless to say, while working for this retailer, I accumulated more home decor and craft supplies than I could ever use or comfortably fit into my home. My husband did not understand my obsession with these sales. I did not always know what I would bring home nor did I always have a plan for what to do with these amazing deals. In my husband's mind, he would rather go to the store and purchase things he needed rather than have an abundance of things taking up valuable space in our home. He believed it was better to purchase the item when you needed it, and possibly pay full price, rather than get a deal and not have a use for something.

Once I found these bargain must-haves, I then needed to find a place to store my treasures. I purchased large shelves to store these items in my garage. However, I did not want to pay full price for storage shelving in my garage. I have been conditioned to wait for a sale and purchase when an item is discounted. I found two shelves that fit the space I needed. One shelf was heavy duty metal shelves and cost $400. Another shelf I found was somewhat smaller and consisted of particle board shelves but only cost $80. The shelves made with particle board were less expensive, and I was drawn to the deal. We were able to save so much money with this choice, and we felt confident in our purchase.

However, after only two years, the particle boards began to warp and became unsafe to store items on the shelves. In retrospect, we may have gotten a better deal in the long run if we opted for the heavy duty metal shelves. After the less expensive shelves gave in, we returned to the store and paid full price for the more durable metal shelves to securely and safely store my prized treasures.

Eventually, I slowly filtered through my amazing sample sale purchases and began to donate unwanted items I once found at deep discounted prices. In the end, I realized I had purchased extra storage and shelving (that broke down) to store these discounted items (that I honestly did not need). However, five years later, the metal shelves are holding strong in our garage and storing more valuable items today that suit my family's needs.

I remember as I embarked into the unknown chapter of parenthood, I was bombarded by advice and advertisements for must haves to make life easier as a mom-to-be. I fell victim to the overwhelming hormones, information, and gadgets that were must-haves for mom and baby. Although a few items I purchased did ease life with a new baby, my sleep deprived body was desperate to find the perfect product to help my son to sleep through the night. I finally found the miracle I had been so desperately searching for in a Velcro swaddle. For anyone that is not a neonatal nurse and has attempted to swaddle a baby, you know how incompetent a piece of fabric can make you feel, especially at three a.m. with a crying infant.

My first-born loved being swaddled at night, and the Velcro swaddles were a *lifesaver* for me, my kid, and my husband. When I was pregnant with my second son, I planned to use these swaddles from the beginning. I was now a master in motherhood and felt confident that I had found the holy grail in fighting sleep deprivation. I shopped for sales at baby stores and stocked up on these sleep-saving miracles. I was very pleased I found such a good deal on these swaddles, saving money while also saving my sanity.

My overconfidence was quickly shattered. I soon learned that my second son was very different from my first. He wanted nothing to do with a swaddle. Kids have a great sense of humor and are able to sabotage the best laid plans. He woke up crying, uncomfortable, and sweating in the middle of the night. Therefore, I would wake up in the middle of the night, crying, uncomfortable, and exhausted. Eventually, I ended up giving these once highly prized swaddles away to another mom and baby who loved them as much as my first son. I am glad the swaddles helped another mom and another child, but the time, money, and hope I spent acquiring these great deals on swaddles was sadly wasted.

Honestly, I would not know what worked for my children unless I was open to trial and error. The challenging part is, I do not usually apply this same mindset with other items in my home. As a mom, I am comfortable and can confidently discard or donate items that I know I or my child are not using. But when it is such a good deal, it is hard to resist the justification of that purchase.

Upon reflection, I feel guilty over my over consumerism that has contributed excess waste to landfills. This is likely why I feel a strong need to donate most things or justify that something still has a use so that I do not feel as much guilt about getting rid of it. Discarding belongings has been a challenge for most of my life. If I truly only purchased items I need and will use, I think I would feel less guilt if and when the item had served its purpose. I continue to search for balance as I navigate the urge to purchase good deals. Focusing on my *needs* and not just my *wants* will encourage me to evaluate my buying habits and refrain from purchasing things I will not use.

REFRAME

"It's not a good deal if you don't need it."
– Anonymous

Courtney

Walking down the clearance aisle or finding a deal online can entice us to spend money on items we typically would not spend money on, do not need, or only need one of in our life. Marketing ploys are smart and also tricky at times. The "Buy three, get one Free!" or items on "clearance," may drive consumers to buy, but in reality, how good of a deal are you getting if the price is marked down only ten percent on clearance? These "bargain deals" trigger our brains to think we are getting a great price and, because of this, we should buy multiple! According to Statista.com, in the United States in 2023, marketing was a billion-dollar industry with digital marketing campaigns in high demand. We are inundated with hundreds of sales pitches and marketing ads daily on television, radio, and online.

The psychology behind marketing attempts to grab the attention of their targeted audience and create an urgency for purchasing. Many market strategies use the "Four V's" – Volume, Velocity, Variety, and Veracity – to capture their targeted audience. The *Volume* or overall content blasted out to the target audience is one strategy that retailers use to capture the target audience's attention. How much information can a retailer send out and get in front of a potential purchaser? Now, with the digital age, it can seem as though we are spammed with advertisements and promotional information each time we turn on the television, drive down the road, or turn on our computer to check email. According to *Forbes* magazine, the number of social media users has exploded to 4.9 billion people globally. Projections for social media marketing are to reach $247.3 billion by 2027. We are daily inundated with mass volumes of marketing ploys, battling to win our dollars and entice us to purchase their products or services.

The *Velocity,* or frequency in which we see an advertisement, also has a large effect on if or when we purchase something. Marketers are masters of this game. The quicker marketing can reach their desired customer base, the better the chances that the customer becomes a purchaser of the services or products. This strategy ensures that new advertisements are sent out quickly and are seen frequently by the target audience. Some companies spend hundreds and thousands of dollars just to ensure that their product or service is seen regularly. Remember that metrics are calculated and information about your demographics, interests, and what you search online are being measured and used to send you advertisements that are intentionally focused on being seen by you, the targeted audience.

The *Variety* of channels that a market can reach also increases the chances that a target audience will become a loyal customer. Television, radio, Facebook, TikTok, email blasts, and Google Ads are different avenues in which advertisers send blasts about their products and services. Seeing advertisements on all of these channels can increase the likelihood that consumers will opt to consume their products and services. Remember that there are algorithms, formulas, and metrics that marketers and social media platforms use to create content and advertisements to target each user and consumer in the market. Just because you see an advertisement on television and social media does not prove that the product or service is reputable or worth the value promised. Do your own research before purchasing the promised deal that you cannot miss.

Lastly, *Veracity* is the measure of perceived relevant and trustworthy content. The veracity of an advertisement can illustrate the validity, relevance, and helpfulness of a product or service to consumers. And consumers want an easy answer, a quick fix and a simple solution to their problems and needs. Marketers promise sunshine, rainbows, fast results, and miracles in their advertisements. However, reviewing online customer ratings, Better Business Bureau reviews, and subscribing to *Consumer Reports* can help you to be a smarter consumer and avoid the trap of the false promises and let downs of the advertised amazing deals.

Consumerism surrounds us all within our culture. According to the Worldwatch Institute in 2019, North America and Western Europe accounted for only twelve percent of the world's population; however, they consume sixty percent of the world's private consumption spending. Whether we are consuming information, entertainment, or window shopping to pass the time, taking in and acquiring more has become a lifestyle for many. Whether you are a young person finding your independence in the world, a middle-aged person focused on career and life advancement, or a grandparent seeking out new and exciting experiences after the workforce, we can all fall victim to over consumption. Americans especially, can fall victim to the consumption craze.

According to *The Daily Mail*, women will spend more than eight years of their lives shopping. However, with life experience, some have learned to navigate and realize what good deals to pass by and what deals to take advantage of in life. Unfortunately, the excitement and adrenaline rush that comes from finding a good deal can be hard for many to resist.

The challenge to battle impulse buying is to slow down and reframe your mindset about spending. Before you go out and snatch up the deal of the century, ask yourself a few questions to ensure that you are really getting a good deal.

- Do I really need or want this item or service?
- If this item were not on sale, would I still consider purchasing the item?
- How many uses will I truly get out of this item (cost per use)?
- Does purchasing this item now delay or impede other goals I have previously established?
- Is this item worth the real estate it is taking up in my home or storage unit?

REFRAMING QUESTIONS

1. Do I have the financial resources to purchase this item or service?
2. Is this an item or service I have planned on purchasing?
3. How likely am I to use this item?
4. How long is this item likely to last or be usable?
5. Is this an item I will use or display regularly?
6. Is this an item I must purchase now or can I purchase at a later date when needed?
7. Do I already have something similar to this item in my home currently?
8. Do I have the physical real estate in my home to store or display this item?

* * * * *

R.E.C.L.A.I.M. Case Study

It's Such a Good Deal

This client is a bargain hunter who searches for good deals to save money on things for herself but also to give back to others who are less fortunate. This client told us, "I don't have a lot, but I can help. It's what we are supposed to do." She purchases coats for children and adults to give away during the cold months and collects toys throughout the year to donate to underprivileged children during the holiday season. Recently, she has expanded her savvy shopping expertise to search out formal wear for teenage girls and young women for special events.

Her passion to help others and give back to the community through coat donations started with donating coats to the homeless over twenty years ago. While she loves a good deal, she believes in quality over quantity. She inspects and verifies the quality of the coat by ensuring the zippers work properly and the linings are intact. She prefers to donate coats to reputable charities, such as homeless shelters and underprivileged schools in her surrounding communities.

In life, she has gone from a three-bedroom, two-bath house to one bedroom in a shared home with an eight-by-ten storage shed. Soon, she hopes to move into her own one-bedroom apartment. Life circumstances have changed along her life journey; however, she has kept her promise to give back, realizing that even a small donation can have a big impact on someone in need. As she prepares to relocate to her own space, she decides to evaluate her storage shed to revisit her belongings that have been in storage for six years. The good deals, kitchenware, home decor, sentimental items, and documents she has continued to store have started to see damage and been compromised in the Texas heat in her storage unit.

Several of the flimsy cardboard boxes are broken and some also have mold starting to grow on the bottom because of the excess humidity. Some items stored in cardboard boxes and plastic containers are broken due to heavy boxes placed on top, causing the lids to buckle. Understanding this client and her needs, we choose to purchase durable storage bins with lids to replace the current warped cardboard boxes and broken plastic storage bins. We hope to preserve and protect the client's belongings stored in the shed to maintain the value of her items. Our goal is to organize her personal items as well as create appropriate space and storage for the items she purchases to donate.

Before we started the Reframe and R.E.C.L.A.I.M. process, we asked a few questions to better understand our client and her perspectives.

What have been the obstacles for you in assessing and evaluating the items you want to address today?
Just seeing how much paperwork I haven't thrown away. I have clothes I haven't worn in years that I can donate. It's depressing because I look at the shed and realize this is what I have left from a three-bedroom, two-bath house that my kids lived in when they were growing up.

How long have you been accumulating the items we will be reviewing today?
Some items I have been storing for forty-six years, since my first child was born. The boxes storing my items in the shed have been stored for six years.

How do you feel now with us here to start the Reframe & Reclaim process?
I'm a little apprehensive. I just want to be done. Doing the process is uncomfortable, so I may give you both a hard time as we are going through things.

Is there anything about this process that you think may be uncomfortable for you?
I just don't want my things to be criticized. I don't want to be criticized. I keep stuff like the clothes my kids wore home from the hospital. I have notes from relatives. To me that's important to keep so my children can see their report cards and little drawings that they made. It's very important to me.

As we start the R.E.C.L.A.I.M. process, we will go through the seven-step process below:

R – REFLECT on the current space.

How is this space currently being used?
Inside my home, I have dresses that I have collected for donation that have been hung up in the entryway, doorways, door frames, and in closet spaces. My storage shed is used as storage for my personal belongings.

What is your hope for the functionality of this space?
I want my home to function the way it is supposed to. I want to have nothing hanging on my doorways or closet doors. I hope to get my doorways back. The dresses need their own space. I want to be able to close my closet doors and have access to my closet. Right now, the dresses are an obstacle I have to go around.

I want to organize the items I collect to donate and have a space to store them so they don't overtake my everyday living space. I want coats, dresses, and toys to be stored in containers or plastic garment bags to protect them. I want it to be a safe, walkable, and inviting space so people don't have to dodge dresses and things. I want it to be more open.

The storage shed needs to be packed better, organized and labeled so I know what is what. I want containers with lids so creepy crawlies can't get in there, and I can preserve my sentimental items. Just to be able to go in and see the items clearly labeled and know where to put them in the new apartment when I move.

How do you hope to feel when you see this space once the Reframe & Reclaim process is complete?
I hope I feel better and more at ease about the things I really want to keep and know they are better preserved. I want them to be labeled so they will stay better preserved.

What's given you the inspiration to start this today?
I have none. I don't want to move, but I know I need to. My family and the upcoming move has helped encourage me. My inspiration is not to take unnecessary items with me in my next move.

E – EVALUATE each item and understand the true value each item has for you as you empty the space. Reimagine how this space functions. *How does each item fit into your aspirational space? Does each item match the feel and function you imagined for the space?*

After the initial interview, we noticed apprehension and some discomfort with the Reframe and R.E.C.L.A.I.M. process. We attempted to reassure the client that we are here to support her and her decision making. We will not be making decisions for her.

We are doing all of the physical work. The decision-making part is mentally taxing and exhausting, which is why people can struggle to begin this process. So, if we can take on the physical work, you can put all your focus and attention on making decisions.

We situate a chair near the storage shed with a table to lay out items for our client to review. We stage and label various boxes and bins to categorize and organize the client's belongings as she evaluates each item. These categories include: Donate, Move to a new apartment, and Items to stay stored in the shed.

As we start the R.E.C.L.A.I.M. process, the client shares that she does not plan to donate many items because she previously filtered through most of her items that she is currently storing. However, she does admit she has a lot of paperwork and documents that she needs to evaluate, shred, and discard.

She shares that she is hopeful to donate her unused items and give them new life with someone that can use and enjoy them. She is especially excited to give her business clothes to organizations that support and educate women recovering from domestic violence. She hopes that her clothing donations will give women another resource and contribute to their confidence in finding new employment and ability to start a new chapter of their lives.

As she begins to evaluate her belongings, she quickly makes decisions about the stored items in her shed. Surprising all of us, the donation pile quickly grows. After only sixteen minutes of reviewing and evaluating her storage shed contents, she chooses to donate three bags of coats, a formal gown, a suitcase full of clothes, home decor, handbags, and a box of housewares. It becomes apparent that she no longer needs or wants many items that have been stored the past six years in her storage shed.

How do you feel?
Okay. I like this. Not all of these belongings are imperative for me to keep and some things won't mean anything to anyone but me. I've gotten to the point really where I don't need all of this stuff. I'm not as materialistic, maybe, as I used to be. I like nice things but I don't have to have anything but a mattress, a comfortable chair, my remote, and batteries for my remote.

We continue to pull items out of the storage shed and find a large suitcase filled with papers. The client finds a few sentimental items to keep but discards and shreds the majority of the documents. Previously, the boxes that will be moving to her new apartment were labeled, but many contain a mixture of items that will live in different rooms of her new apartment. We use our newly purchased heavy-duty containers to organize her items by location for her upcoming relocation. When she does move, it will be helpful to view the labeled bins and relocate them to the appropriate rooms in her new apartment.

We eventually come across two bags of toys the client has previously purchased at a great deal and collected for donation. Along with the toys she hopes to donate to children, she keeps a collection of items she has purchased on sale including: stickers, toys, and other items she thinks her grandchildren might want to play with. We come across a bag full of several stickers and Halloween decorations she purchased at a great deal. She originally intended for these items to be distributed to her grandchildren, but has not yet. The client easily decides to donate these items so someone will be able to use them.

The client shares that she has misplaced or forgotten items she collects throughout the year to donate or gift to others. Her memory is sparked as she evaluates her belongings in storage. As we work our way through her storage shed, the client becomes excited, finding her Bible that has been packed away for six years.

Client: I'm so thankful I found my large print Bible. This is going inside with me.

She is able to reclaim several items she has misplaced or forgotten about including a hat, gifts from her grandson, several family photos, and a sketchbook full of drawings she drew when she was eleven years old.

Two hours into the evaluation stage, we take a lunch break and discuss with the client her perspective thus far with the Reframe and R.E.C.L.A.I.M. process.

Client: I feel like I'm on the *Hoarders* TV show. No, *Storage Wars*. I appreciate your help. I hope people can enjoy and use the items I'm donating. It feels good because it's stuff I don't need. It's stuff I haven't needed. I'm going to have a cleaner, more efficient, and functional apartment. Look at all this stuff I don't have to move or pay someone to move. It's a lot of stuff I have already chosen to donate, and we're only two hours in. I thought it would take all frickin' day!

You said you didn't have a lot to donate but we have a whole car full already.
I have enough stuff to have a yard sale.

After lunch, we return to the storage shed to continue the evaluation process.

We find a large container of clothing. In the matter of minutes, the client chooses to donate the majority of the items. Several garments still have the original price tags attached and have never been worn.

In total, we evaluated one large suitcase and a large storage container filled with clothing. The client chooses to donate over eighty items of clothes. After evaluating all of the clothing donations, we realize that more than twenty items of the clothes the client has been storing in her storage shed for six years have the original sales tags intact. The client is proud to find many of these items on sale or for a good deal; however, because these clothes have not yet been worn, the money spent on the good deals has gone to waste.

During the initial interview with this client, she spoke about the importance of her sentimental items stored in her shed. She comes across a plastic bin with a handmade quilt inside. She tells us her grandmother made this quilt for her and she wants to keep it. Later, she comes across a spiral bound cookbook that belonged to the same grandmother, and she decides to donate it.

Throughout the evaluation process, the client is becoming more discerning about what items to keep for sentimentality and other items that she is not strongly connected to today. She is finding momentum in the process with our support and facilitation, thinking critically about her next phase of life and quickly and confidently making decisions about her belongings. Three hours into the R.E.C.L.A.I.M. process, a family member joins the conversation and begins to look through the large donation pile.

Family Member: Are you having a garage sale?
Client: No. It's all going to be dropped off today for donation.

Family Member: You're getting rid of these dominoes? These are the really good kind.
Client: I already have another set. I don't need two.

Family Member: You could make something out of that material. Don't get rid of that.
Client: Donate it.

Family Member: You're getting rid of these? Some of these are worth fifteen dollars.

Client: I know. I don't want them. Once we go through the rest of my things, you can decide what you want to keep from the donation pile.

Since returning from lunch, the client evaluates the remaining ten boxes and containers in her storage unit. This last segment of evaluation took a total of forty minutes. We are all surprised by the decisiveness of the client and how she changes from apprehension at the beginning of the day to comfort in trusting the R.E.C.L.A.I.M. process as the day progresses.

Client: It feels good seeing all the things I'm going to donate. Somebody can use it. You know, somebody that actually wears that size clothing.

How does it feel seeing the items you have decided to keep?
Good. I unloaded a lot. There is less to move. There is less to find space for in my one-bedroom, 600-square-foot apartment. So, I think everything is going to fit well, and I don't have to go through it again before my move.

C – CLEAN the space. Empty and clean the space so that it feels like a fresh, clean slate.

How do you feel seeing this space empty versus how you felt with the space occupied with items?
I was really surprised with how much I got rid of and how much more space I have to use. I could maybe live in the shed. It looks great.

L – LAYOUT and label the space before placing any items back into the space. Attempt to create a blueprint of how the space will look and feel. Measure and readjust the space to fit the space's new functionality, as well as any organizational materials that you may include to enhance the aesthetic and functionality.

What do you hope this space will be for you now that you have reflected and evaluated the items in this space and the space's function?
My main hope is that everything is in proper containers and covered so that my things are protected. Some of the picture frames were compromised but the photos were still good so I will reframe those photos.

A – ASSEMBLE items back into the space and adjust as needed. Allow for trial and error as you reimagine the space's blueprint. This may be adjusting materials, changing where items are located or reframing what items are truly intended for this new environment.

We reassemble the storage shed by separating and categorizing her items into three categories: items that are moving with her to her new apartment, items that are staying in the storage shed, and boxes of personal documents she will evaluate at a later time. For the items that she has chosen to keep, the contents are re-boxed with other similar items in large durable plastic bins with locking lids. These heavy duty bins will better protect and preserve her stored items.

The newly packed containers are then labeled individually by the like contents within each bin, i.e., Kitchenware, Home Decor, Linens, etc. Labels are placed on multiple sides of each container when reassembled in her storage shed so that the labels are easily found and contents can be accessed if needed. To maintain the integrity of all of the contents stored in the new containers, boxes that contain fragile items are also labeled so that heavy boxes will not be stored on top.

Inside the storage shed, the boxes are sorted and stored according to the needs of the client. All containers that will be moved to her new apartment are easily accessed on one side of her storage shed. The boxes of personal documents are on the opposite side of the storage shed on shelves. This creates easy visibility and access to her belongings when the client chooses to evaluate the contents of these boxes. The bins that store all of the items that will remain in her storage shed are stored under the shelves that contain the documents. We hope that this organization system will improve the client's ability to locate all of her belongings when needed in the future.

I – INSPECT the space once everything is reassembled. Step back and take inventory, viewing the aesthetic and functionality of the newly reimagined space. This is the final gut check.

After the assembly process is complete, we invite the client to review the organizational system and inspect the final layout of her storage shed.

Client: I have so much more usable room. It is more organized. It will be easier to load when I move. The functionality is so much be better. It's easy to access. I know exactly where everything is.

Does this space now match the intention you imagined?
Yes, it does. It's going to be easier to move and store things when I move into the apartment. I can store the items in the bins until I need them later, like heavy blankets for the winter. I am very happy.

Does this space now fit your space's function and your current lifestyle needs?
Yes, plus I have more space to store things in the shed. The toys I am going to donate at Christmas are now stored properly in a plastic bin with a lid so they won't get damaged or dirty.

M – MAINTAIN your space. Remember that this space will only stay as organized and aesthetically pleasing as you put effort and intentionality into it. Create a plan and a system to purposefully maintain this new space, recruiting any other people needed that utilize or enjoy this space. Accountability is key.

As we neared the end of the seven- step R.E.C.L.A.I.M. process with this client, we wanted to ensure that our client had awareness and a plan of action to continue to maintain this beautiful space she had helped to create for her home.

What do you ask yourself to determine what you really need to keep and what to let go of?
If I haven't worn it or used it in years, I don't need it. If my kids haven't read a children's book I saved in thirty years, we probably don't need it. But I'm really happy I found my Bible.

What steps will you need to take to assure that this space will continue to function and feel like it does right now?
Keep everybody out! Honestly, just following the steps we used today. Get appropriate storage bins with lids if I need to store more stuff. Then, just keep what I really need and use.

How do you feel continuing to search for good deals? How will it be different now that you have gone through the R.E.C.L.A.I.M. process?
I'm always going to continue collecting coats and toys. I will just put them in containers until I can donate them. I will limit space to four storage bins. However, I have to stop buying formal dresses. I just don't have the space.

In the end, the R.E.C.L.A.I.M. process took four hours to complete. In total, twenty-one cardboard boxes, storage containers, and suitcases were evaluated. As we began this process, the client claimed she "didn't have a lot of stuff to donate." However, as she leaned into the process, trusted herself, and reflected about her next transition, she realized she had more belongings than she needed for this new chapter of life. Her decision to donate several items will allow her to provide resources and support to others in need, something she is passionate about. In total, she donated six large boxes of household items, three bags of coats, a suitcase filled with clothes, a wedding gown, and twenty-four formal gowns.

That afternoon, we donated the coats and dresses she purchased for a great deal to organizations that accept donations year round. Additionally, a heavy duty storage bin is located in her storage shed to collect the toys that she purchases on sale for Christmas donations.

We also want to evaluate how our client experienced the seven steps of R.E.C.L.A.I.M. We asked her the following questions:

How did you feel during the process? We can see from your body language this morning in the interview compared to your body language now that you are more relaxed.
I felt better than I expected. Y'all did a lot of work, and I appreciate it. I found some things that have been missing. My move is going to go a lot faster, easier, and be more organized. Having proper storage and containers with lids is a big thing. No more soggy bottom boxes and issues.

Was the R.E.C.L.A.I.M. process what you expected it to be?
No. It was better than I anticipated. The process was a lot faster, actually. I thought it would have taken two to three days to complete, and we finished in four hours. We did well.

Do you feel comfortable to continue this process now that you have experienced it today?
Yes, I need to go through my closet. I can go through my winter clothes and donate my career clothes.

What advice do you have for others that are unsure about starting or just beginning this process?
Just let them do it. There are many other people that need the things that you do not need or want. Don't keep and accumulate your things. Let stuff go so that other people that really need things have more resources. Plus, you are not bogged down and just storing things for no reason.

Is there anything about the process you would change?
No. It worked really well. Thank you for helping. I really dreaded it. But I'm glad it's over. Do I have time for a nap?

FOLLOW-UP

We contact the client after her move to her new space. When we began this process, the client was very apprehensive and not motivated to begin the R.E.C.L.A.I.M. process. We were eager to hear more about her experience since we last met.

Now that you've lived with the system for a few months how does it feel?
It feels great! I am relieved that I was able to get rid of so much excess. I had less stuff to move when I moved to my new place. My things were more organized and able to move in a more timely and efficient manner.

Does it still work? Anything you would change?
It worked well for me to help me prepare for my move. I would not change anything.

Do you have any regrets about letting go of any of your items?
Absolutely not. I had an overabundance of things that I kept but did not need. It felt relieving to purge all of the excess stuff. I was able to give clothes I did not need to others so that they could use them. Giving to those in need is something that I feel everyone should do.

How has this process helped you reframe your relationship with your things?
I am going to keep my belongings to a minimum as much as I can, because I realize that I do not need that much. I have plenty. Before, there was so much excess. I will walk by something in the store and if I do not need it, I will not buy it. Because now I realize how much stuff I purchased and did not need or use. I feel guilty by accumulating so much stuff and not using it. I had a lot of

clothes that I chose to donate that still had tags on them and I never wore. I am already saving a lot of money and will continue to save through this learning process. It has given me a different mindset that I do not want to accumulate clutter or unnecessary things, but now I am saving money by not buying things that I do not need. That is a big difference for me. I am very appreciative of going through the R.E.C.L.A.I.M. process and helping me to sort my life out a little better. I am going to keep my life sorted.

Have you started to evaluate any other spaces in your home since your first R.E.C.L.A.I.M. process with us?
Yes. I have created so much more closet space by continuing to go through my clothes. I was able to donate two large garbage bags of clothes from my bedroom closet alone. I want to look through my kitchen supplies next now that I am in my new space. As I unpack my belongings in my new space, I am excited to continue to purge and give to those in need. I want to make my space more livable for me.

* * * * *

For Your Personal R.E.C.L.A.I.M. Process

Purchasing items because they are on sale or seem to be a great deal is a healthy and positive way to use your finances wisely. A problem arises when the impulse to purchase an item on sale overrides the likely usefulness of the item. To avoid this pitfall, use the following strategies to help you purchase with intention and purpose and not impulse buy because you cannot pass up a good deal.

PLAN BEFORE YOU PURCHASE

Before purchasing anything new for your home or wardrobe, we recommend taking the following steps.

- Take the time to research and brainstorm your ideal home aesthetic, wardrobe, or organizational system.
- Create a vision board or mood board using images from magazines or online resources such as Pinterest or Canva, reflecting your focus and intentions for your needs and goals.
- Take a photo or screenshot of the vision board or mood board to have with you when you go shopping.
- Refer to your vision board or mood board before jumping at a good deal that does not truly meet your need or function of your home or space. A great deal may be a financial steal, but also not be the best deal for your personal wants or needs.
- Focus on your personal goals to ensure your time and financial resources are being utilized in the best way. Waiting for the right fit for you will be more rewarding than finding something that is on sale but not what you truly want or need.
- This strategy can help you focus your attention, time, and financial resources to achieve the plan you desire.

INVEST IN QUALITY OVER QUANTITY

Life is too short to tolerate mediocre. Purchase more durable and quality-made items in lieu of multiple lesser quality items. For example, purchase one quality pair of shoes in lieu of three pairs of less quality and less durable shoes. Or choose to purchase heavy duty durable storage bins, ensuring the protection of your items to be stored instead of using cardboard boxes that can easily damage and break down.

If possible, save money and resources to purchase items that are longer lasting and meet your needs. To achieve your goals, create a timeline and budget to purchase what you want or need instead of purchasing items that are a quick fix. Are you purchasing bargain items that you will rarely use? If you choose to resist the urge to purchase items that are "a good deal," could the money saved be used to purchase a more quality item that you will use more frequently? Life is too short to add another unused or nonfunctional item to your home that will most likely end up in a landfill.

COST PER USE

Another popular strategy to evaluate the return on your investment and analyze how good of a good deal you are truly getting is to calculate the cost per use. In the fashion industry this is called cost per wear. However, this strategy can be modified to fit any item. Calculating the cost per use before you purchase an item can help you realize the item's true cost and help you decide if the value is worth the purchase price. See an example below to calculate.

TOTAL COST / NUMBER OF TIMES USED = COST PER USE

For example, you purchase two shirts to wear over the next year. You find a great deal for shirt number one, paying only $10.00. Shirt number two is a shirt you choose to pay full price for, $50.00.

If you wear shirt number one only one time during the year, the cost per use is $10.00. $10.00 total divided by 1 use = $10.00 per use.

If you wear shirt number two every other week, the cost per use is $1.92.
$50.00 total divided by 26 uses = $1.92 per use.

Reframing how you spend your money and how you use your purchases is a helpful way to understand the total value of each item rather than just the purchase price of each item. It is less expensive to purchase the $10.00 shirt; however, you may wear the higher priced shirt more often and be able to wear it for a longer period of time if the quality of the shirt is better than the bargain shirt. Reframing your mindset and spending habits can help you make a smarter investment in your daily spending habits.

There is no wrong or right answer to your purchasing choices. Only you can decide what spending habits and budgets are best for you. For some, the $10.00 shirt may be worn fifty times over the span of a year. This adds up to be a truly great deal, costing only twenty cents per use. Evaluating how much use or wear you will get out of an item can be helpful in reframing the cost per use and overall value of an item. Would you rather get a bargain of a deal on an item that you minimally like but love the price tag, or would you rather spend more money on an item that you know you love and will use regularly in your home?

BE AWARE OF PEER PRESSURE PURCHASING

Having a good friend or family member as a sounding board and purchasing assistant can be fun and helpful; however, be aware of peer pressure purchasing. If someone gives you advice to make a purchase because it is something you cannot pass up, ask yourself if you also love the item in question or if you feel pressured to purchase it. In the end, it is your pocket book, your closet, your home's real estate, and your belongings. If you do not truly love the item in question, be brave to speak up and think about the purchase overnight or longer if needed. A sale item is amazing, but only if you think the item on sale is also amazing! Spending money on a sale is not really money saved if you do not end up using, wearing, or enjoying the item in the first place. Mediocrity has no place in your home. Be sure to choose what items *you* want, need, and choose to take home rather than be pressured by others to make a purchase because *they* think it is a good idea.

Remembering to plan before you purchase can be a helpful strategy when you feel pressured by others to purchase. If someone else is shopping and purchasing items, do not feel pressured to also purchase to go along with the crowd. Focusing your mindset on specific items you are looking for, wanting in your home, and need for yourself can be a helpful tool to practice intentional spending habits. If you still find it hard to resist the urge when everyone else is choosing to spend their money, you may have to decide to remove yourself from the situations that derail you from your goals.

If "It's such a good deal" strikes a chord with you and you are ready to take action in your space, reference the Tips for Your Personal Reframe & R.E.C.L.A.I.M. Process at the end of our book.

CHAPTER 5

IT HAS VALUE

*"I'm not aging.
I'm just increasing my value like a rare collectible."*
– Anonymous

Jennifer

As I continued my personal reflection about my mindset and connection to my things, I also continued analyzing my family's behaviors. I realized that we all shared another common perspective – keeping an item because of its possible value… one day. I do not know how many times I have heard, *This could be worth something someday!* I am convinced that this phrase alone is the reason my mother loves the television show *Antiques Roadshow*. Just like the individuals featured on the show, we believed that in the midst of all our bargains and knick-knacks, we owned a hidden treasure that was worth one hundred times the purchase price. The thrill and surprise we felt watching this show gave us hope that our simple treasures could also be evaluated and appraised for an outrageous dollar amount.

When I visited my maternal grandparents in the summers, my grandfather always let me pick out a few tchotchkes he purchased at the local church bazaars and flea markets. As a kid, I chose the items that looked interesting and cute to me. One time, I chose a glass candy dish that reminded me of a shiny genie lamp. My grandfather commented that I had good taste choosing this item, and my developing brain held tight to that sentiment. Was this candy dish more valuable than the other items I had chosen before? What was different and special about this item? I still keep this candy dish hidden away and unused because maybe it is more valuable than some of the other items I collected. I was told for years that this item was high quality and valuable, but upon further research, I discovered it was being sold for anywhere from $22.00 to $50.00. I do not know how much my grandfather paid for the glass candy dish, but if I do not love it and use it, is the square footage that I devote to this item worth the cost of storing it in my living room sideboard for the past thirty-five years?

In my early twenties. I was a budding designer growing up in the beginning era of DIY. I religiously watched the television show *Trading Spaces*. I loved the instant gratification of transforming a space and seeing the different, albeit sometimes way-out-of-the-box, ideas, and aesthetics. Watching shows like these gave me great joy and inspiration. I especially loved the carpentry work completed by Ty Pennington.

Each year, Fredericks of Hollywood, a lingerie store that was popular in the 1990s and 2000s, hosted a charity fundraiser where celebrities designed a signature corset for auction. In 2004, Ty Pennington designed a corset that was made from thin layered balsa wood shingles, an interesting lingerie choice, but an ode to the DIY carpentry he was well known for creating. Essentially, the corset looked like the siding of a shingle-style home. It was not at all wearable, but it stood out from the other celebrity designs. I bid on this unique piece and fortunately took this wood shingle corset design home. I proudly displayed my prize in a shadowbox in my home office.

Now, twenty years later, I still have the wood shingle corset in the shadowbox, but it has been stored away for nine years. Ty would be *SO* disappointed. I still love this unique item, but the aesthetics of my home has changed since I claimed this prize. I was in my twenties when I admired and displayed my Ty Pennington corset. Now, I have a husband, two boys and less wall space to display this item. Instead, my home is focused around my boys' activities, holiday decorations, and family memories. Why do I still have this item if I no longer display it? Well, because it just might be worth something someday.

Typically, I am very frugal. I have even been called cheap. I value finding a good deal, but I also believe in paying more for quality if the item is something I will use frequently. For example, I will pay more for luggage that will stand the test during my travel; for cars that have reputations for functionality, dependability, and value; and for timeless furniture that will stand up to the energy of my boys. However, for everyday items that come and go, I do not see the point in spending a lot of money. I do not follow trendy new fashions. Instead, I prefer to wear solid-colored basics that are versatile. But if I see something that I really like and can justify the cost per wear, I will spend more money on that item.

In the past, I have splurged or been given more expensive items. I tended to put more costly items on a pedestal, deeming these items luxurious and more valuable than my less expensive items. Mentally, I know that all items are purchased to be used and enjoyed, but I tell myself they are too special. I give them an inflated value that makes the item so important that I tell myself I have to wait for a special occasion to use it or not to use it at all. In reality, the inflated value is only in my mind.

For example, when it comes to bath and spa products, I mentally label these as "luxury" and tell myself that these items are only reserved for special occasions. Usually, it is either because the item is discontinued and no longer made or I just really, really like it. But when a special occasion does arise, and I have met the "special occasion" criteria, I still tend to tell myself that I will save the luxury item for a "more special" occasion.

Over time, these items I claim for "luxury" get stored away in a cabinet and moved from home to home over the years. Eventually, the very special occasions I wait for to use these valuable items never come to fruition. Instead, my bath and spa items go to waste and expire. The oils separate in my creamy lotion and the candle scent I love fades. Not only do these products go to waste, I have also wasted the real estate used to store the items that will never be used. When all is said and done, I have wasted the valuable money spent on these products and forfeited the joy of using these items. I continue to find it challenging to use these luxury products because I do not typically spend large amounts of money on myself. Because of this, I do not want to use these luxury items just any day.

An example of this dilemma occurred in 2015, when I ran the Disney Marathon. I bought an exclusive pair of limited edition New Balance "run Disney" shoes. When the shoes are released, they are only available for purchase at the Disney Expo before the race. Most shoes are sold out in the first few hours. I was fortunate to purchase the Cinderella-themed shoes with golden-yellow ribbon shoe laces. These light-blue shoes stand out from all of my other running shoes, and when worn, display my badge of honor to be part of the exclusive Disney running community. However, if I wear these coveted shoes, there is a chance for them to get scuffed and dirty or possibly ruined. I must now ask myself if it is worth the risk of wearing these highly prized shoes or do I store this valuable purchase away in my closet. Is keeping the shoes in my closet a waste of real estate if I choose to never wear the Disney Cinderella Shoes?

In addition to items I purchase myself, I also have great friends and family who have gifted me some very nice items. Some of these gifted items are so valuable, in fact, that I never use them out of fear I will ruin or break them. The desire to preserve these valuable items is greater than the risk of using them. Therefore, I never use them, they stay stored and tucked away, and I waste the limited available real estate on items I may never use.

My good friend gave me a gorgeous set of ombre crystal martini glasses from New York City. Each glass is a different color that fades to clear. They are delicate, beautiful and stored away safely for special occasions. However, when a special occasion arises, I rarely bring them out because I do not want them to break. Therefore, I have been carrying these crystal glasses for twenty-one years and have used them only two or three times.

For my valued and adored items, I really need to evaluate each to decide their true value for me. Evaluating the personal value rather than the monetary value is something that I have learned to reframe for myself. Fearful preservation does not allow me to personally enjoy and value items, but I have to make a conscious effort not to fall back into this negative mindset. I ask myself the following questions to help keep my personal values of each item in perspective: *What if I use the item and it breaks? If I were given the choice, would I replace this item if it were damaged? If there were a fire, would I choose to grab this item before racing to safety?* For me, I now attempt to love and use, display or share my belongings rather than keep my belongings tucked away and wasting away.

<u>REFRAME</u>

"The problem: we put more value on our stuff than on our space."
– Frencine Jay

Courtney

The idea of something growing in value or worth is exciting! We walk through museums of historical and priceless content, enjoy movies where the main character finds a valuable lost artifact, and dream of one-day cashing in on that family heirloom that pays for our retirement. The catch for some is that they are always on the hunt for the lost relic, unique artifact, or priceless piece of art. When we allow items of potential value to collect in our physical real estate, we do not allow the actual value of the item to be realized. The value of an item is subjective, depending on who you ask.

According to Sofi.com, the monetary value of an item is dependent on multiple factors including rarity, condition of the item, and the demand or market for the specific item. Because of this, some things that one person may consider trash can truly become someone else's treasure. However, the financial payout can vary depending on who the buyer is and what their personal investment may be in having this object in their possession. As of 2024, some of the most highly sought out and paid for valuables include first edition vintage comic books in mint condition, sports memorabilia including baseball cards, vintage bakeware, and rare coins (Sofi.com). For these items, the right buyer will pay generously for an object in perfect condition, however, it takes research of the collector market and authentication for a true collector to seek out and purchase one of these rare finds.

The Endowment Effect is an interesting theory of psychology and economics. Most people will overvalue an object that they own more than something that is not in their possession. This value can be driven by sentimentality, emotional attachment, or the time and energy someone has invested in a belonging. Interestingly, the owner of the object in question typically will overestimate the monetary value of an object while the potential buyer of this object may calculate a different and lesser valuation. For the buyer, there is no emotional connection, yet. But if the buyer is searching for the last missing piece to their long invested in collection, the buyer may also over pay for this object due to their personal time and energy seeking out the object.

Before purchasing an item, it may be helpful to consider or analyze the opportunity cost to understand the true value of an item to you. An opportunity cost is the decision to pass up a purchase in lieu of an alternative purchase or opportunity. Prioritizing your financial goals as well as your overall lifestyle goals can help a buyer to decide what is most important to them. Is the object in question worth the financial cost to the buyer? Does the decision to forego a purchase allow for other valuable opportunities for the buyer? Choosing to pass on the purchase of the rare coin can possibly allow you the opportunity to enjoy a nice dinner with your partner. Passing on the purchase of the fast food lunch every day at work may afford you the opportunity to more quickly save up for the outfit you have been wanting, and benefit you to pass up on the extra calories to look amazing in the jeans you love. This strategy can help many to make more financial sound decisions as well as improve decision making in other areas of their lives.

For the average Joe, it can be helpful to do research to find if your estimated value of the item is worth its weight in gold or just another keepsake that is old. If you are truly interested in learning how to search out and find valuables as a hobby or for a side hustle, there are many resources available online as well as professional appraisers that can be contracted to give you an honest value. But for those of us who only hold onto our precious possible treasures without the honest due diligence to seek out a true market or auction valuation of an object, we may be holding our breath for a payout that will not materialize.

Reframing your mentality surrounding the value of an item can better help you to navigate what is truly valuable, sentimentally or monetarily, and what will continue to take up physical real estate in your home or storage unit. What may be valuable to you, may not be valuable to another person. Ask yourself some questions to better decipher what your next steps will be to enjoy your belongings or seek out an appraisal for your treasures. Honestly, what is the price you are paying each day, month, or year in order to keep, store, or display this item in your possession?

REFRAMING QUESTIONS

1. Do I have the financial resources to purchase this item or service?
2. Is this an item or service I have planned on purchasing?
3. How likely am I to use this item?
4. How long is this item likely to last or be usable?
5. Is this an item I will use or display regularly?
6. Is this an item I must purchase now or can I purchase at a later date when needed?
7. Do I already have something similar to this item in my home currently?
8. Do I have the physical real estate in my home to store or display this item?

* * * * *

R.E.C.L.A.I.M. Case Study

It Has Value

The client is a forty-something-year-old that lives with her husband and young child. She has begun the declutter process to create more functional space within her home. Since having her child, she has found that her space easily becomes overfilled and overcrowded by things that are collected by her, her husband, and her child. In attempts to relieve the stress of keeping up her home, she is beginning to reflect and filter through her belongings.

During the decluttering process, she has come across collectible dolls that her grandmother gifted to her as a young child. When she visited her grandmother as a child, she would see the dolls kept behind glass doors in a curio cabinet in her grandmother's home. Her grandmother allowed her to sit with the dolls and hold them under her grandmother's supervision; however, her grandmother told her that the dolls were too valuable to be toys. When the client turned twelve years old, the grandmother allowed the client to take the dolls home if she promised to take good care of them. Being gifted the dolls was a special moment for the client, and she has attempted to preserve the dolls since they were gifted to her.

Unfortunately, her grandmother passed away in 2020, and the client does not know how she acquired these dolls. She does know that her grandmother loved to travel. It is possible that her grandmother purchased these dolls overseas. The dolls still have the certificates of authentication attached including the signature of the doll maker on the certificate. Her grandmother enjoyed collecting many things in her lifetime including playing cards, stationery, hats, jewelry, and had a small collection of dolls.

Since the client was twelve years old, she has kept these dolls safely and carefully boxed up and stored away in her closet for over thirty years in an attempt to preserve their value. She has not looked to have the dolls appraised since they have been in her possession; however, after many years of storing these dolls safely, she is ready to find out more about the dolls and in hopes to find someone who will appreciate the dolls, regardless of their monetary value.

Before we started the Reframe and R.E.C.L.A.I.M. process, we asked a few questions to better understand our client and her perspectives.

What have been the obstacles for you in assessing and evaluating the items you want to address today?
I did not know how to find an honest value for my dolls. Also, I have felt some responsibility to find someone that will appreciate these dolls like my grandmother asked me to appreciate them.

How do you feel when you see this space today?
I feel sad that they have been stored at the top of my closet. They are all packed away in a cardboard box and have been for most of my life. My grandmother loved these dolls, but I do not have the same admiration for them because I rarely took them down, hoping to keep their value preserved.

How do you feel now with us here to start the Reframe & Reclaim process?
I have mixed feelings. I feel relieved that I may find out the dolls' values, but I am unsure what I want to do with them once I find that out. Part of me wants to keep them still, but I know they will only continue to be stored away. I honestly hope to find someone who will appreciate them as much as my grandmother did.

As we start the R.E.C.L.A.I.M. process, we will go through the seven-step process below:

R- REFLECT on the current space.

How is this space currently being used?
The dolls are being stored safely in my closet on a shelf.

What is your hope for the functionality of this space?
I honestly want my closet to continue to function as a space that will store and hold things that I need, but I feel that I need to filter through and narrow down what I truly need in this space. It feels crowded, and my dolls are stored at the top in a corner.

How do you hope to feel when you see this space once the Reframe & Reclaim process is complete?
Only my husband and I really see our closet space, but I hope that we both feel confident we can find the things we are looking for easily. I want the space to function for storage, but I also want the space to not feel overcrowded.

What are your hopes in going through the editing and decluttering process?
I am only focusing on my dolls now. My biggest hope is that I can find someone who will appreciate these dolls like my grandmother did. I have been too afraid to take them down because I do not want them to get dirty or damaged. I want my dolls to find a home where they will be admired, not packed away in a box.

What's given you the inspiration to start this today?
My grandmother passed away three years ago. I am not sentimentally attached to the dolls. I have other things and memories that connect me with my grandmother, but the thought that these dolls are just sitting in my closet upsets me. I want to honor my grandmother by finding someone who will admire these dolls like she did.

E – EVALUATE each item and understand the true value each item has for you as you empty the space. Reimagine how this space functions. *How does each item fit into your aspirational space? Does each item match the feel and function you imagined for the space?*

The client begins by taking a 12"x14" cardboard box down from the top shelf of her closet. The dolls are all stored together in the same box. Two dolls are Gustel Wied dolls from the 1980s, made by Eva-Marie Reick. Another doll is a collectible made by Lee Middleton. This first moments sleeping baby doll with a forget-me-not face is vintage from 1983. The client chooses to research about her keepsake dolls in an attempt to find out more about their history and their value. She contacts two antique appraisers to have an honest appraisal, if possible. Unfortunately, the appraisers report that dolls are not in high demand for collectors and recommend that the client choose to sell her dolls personally online.

The client searches online for the certificates and authenticates each doll's identity. She finds similar dolls to her Gustel Wied dolls for sale on eBay ranging from $25.00 to $48.00 each. The Lee Middleton doll is also found online for a valuation of $30.00 to $70.00. In finding more information about the dolls' values, the client is somewhat disappointed that the dolls are not valued as highly as her grandmother told her, but she is also relieved that she does not feel obligated to continue to store the gifted dolls in her possession for years to come. After thirty years of holding onto the dolls, the client is ready to find a new home for the dolls so that they can be admired, rather than stored away in a closet.

First, the client contacts her two aunts about the dolls, asking if either has any sentimental connection to the dolls before taking action to re-home them. One aunt agrees to keep two of the dolls. The client makes arrangements to pack and ship these two dolls to her aunt for safe keeping. The client's sister was also gifted a Lee Middleton doll when she was a child and she agrees to keep the coordinating doll. She is relieved that the dolls will stay within her family.

C – CLEAN the space. Empty and clean the space so that it feels like a fresh, clean slate.

How do you feel seeing this space empty versus how you felt with the space occupied with items?
It feels sad seeing the small space that these dolls have lived in for at least four years in this home. But I also feel lighter seeing that there is now more empty space in my closet.

L – LAYOUT and label the space before placing any items back into the space. Attempt to create a blueprint of how the space will look and feel. Measure and readjust the space to fit the space's new functionality, as well as any organizational materials that you may include to enhance the aesthetic and functionality.

What do you hope this space will be for you now that you have reflected and evaluated the items in this space and the space's function?
I hope that the small space that has been emptied in my closet will not get crowded again with other things. Maybe I will continue to reclaim more of my closet shelves so that it feels lighter, and I will feel lighter when I walk into my closet space.

A – ASSEMBLE items back into the space and adjust as needed. Allow for trial and error as you reimagine the space's blueprint. This may be adjusting materials, changing where items are located or reframing what items are truly intended for this new environment.

The client chooses to keep the section of the shelf that once stored the dolls clear and empty for the time being. She hopes that she will have the momentum and motivation to continue to declutter her closet shelves and create more open space in her walk-in closet. The closet space that was once used for storage for the dolls will not be assembled for this client.

I – INSPECT the space once everything is reassembled. Step back and take inventory, viewing the aesthetic and functionality of the newly reimagined space. This is the final gut check.

Does this space now fit your space's function and your current lifestyle needs?
Yes. I feel relief that my closet space has been reclaimed and that my dolls will have a new home with someone who will admire them.

M – MAINTAIN your space. Remember that this space will only stay as organized and aesthetically pleasing as you put effort and intentionality into it. Create a plan and a system to purposefully maintain this new space, recruiting any other people needed that utilize or enjoy this space. Accountability is key.

As we neared the end of the seven-step R.E.C.L.A.I.M. process with this client, we wanted to ensure that our client had awareness and a plan of action to continue to maintain this beautiful space she had helped to create for her home.

What system will you put in place to keep this space as you see it today?

I think that I will ask myself if I truly need or want something stored in my closet. Will I really use it or need it later?

We also want to evaluate how our client experienced the seven steps of R.E.C.L.A.I.M. We asked her the following questions:

How did you feel during the process?

I was comfortable and curious. I did not feel pressured to make a decision about the dolls. When I found out how much the dolls are valued in the collector world, I was disappointed and relieved. My grandmother told me the dolls were valuable. And maybe they were at one time or maybe she thought they could be valuable one day. However, the dolls are valued between $25.00 - $75.00 each. I am relieved that they are not worth more because I wanted to find someone who would appreciate them. If they had more monetary value, I may have felt pressure or obligation to keep them stored in my closet for safe keeping. I now feel comfortable and confident to gift them to my family members.

Was the R.E.C.L.A.I.M. process what you expected it to be?
Yes, I was hopeful to reclaim my space and re-home the dolls, but I was unsure where to start to find the value of the dolls. I was surprised that the antique dealers and appraisers were not interested in giving me a valuation.

Do you feel comfortable to continue this process now that you have experienced it today?
Yes. I hope I will continue with my closet now that I have started.

What space do you hope to evaluate next?
My walk-in closet then maybe my clothes in my dresser.

What advice do you have for others that are unsure about starting or just beginning this process?
I recommend having someone to keep you accountable. It is challenging to navigate this process by yourself. I was thankful to have you to help me find answers and get started with rehoming my dolls.

Is there anything about the process you would change?
No. I was happy with the outcome.

Any feedback you have for us as we have helped you facilitate this process?
Thank you for your support and encouragement throughout the process. I have felt that I needed to give these dolls the opportunity to be appreciated and enjoyed. I am thankful that this process was the catalyst to finally do that.

FOLLOW-UP

We contacted this client after she completed the R.E.C.L.A.I.M. process to check in with her and hear more about her closet space. We were curious about her experience and how she feels now after she made the decision to part with the dolls gifted to her from her grandmother. We asked her the following questions below.

Now that you've lived with the system for a few months how does it feel?
It feels good that the closet space has been opened up, but most importantly, I am happy that my family has chosen to keep the dolls and appreciate them.

Do you have any regrets about letting go of any of your items?
No, especially since my family members will now have the dolls. I trust my family to appreciate the dolls since they were originally my grandmother's. I am happy that the dolls will be in the family.

How has this process helped you reframe your relationship with your things?
I am not sure if this process has changed my mindset about things, but I think I now have more insight and understanding of how to find the value of my belongings in the future if needed. Hopefully, I will not wait thirty years to research items and learn more about them.

Have you started to evaluate any other spaces in your home since your first R.E.C.L.A.I.M. process with us?
I started to evaluate my clothes in my closet. I pulled out clothes that no longer fit and offered the clothes to other family members and donated the remaining. I am still working through my closet slowly, but I hope to tackle the entire closet soon.

* * * * *

For Your Personal R.E.C.L.A.I.M. Process

Evaluating and understanding your personal connection and felt value for an object is the first step in making decisions about your belongings. Before researching the monetary value of an object in the market, reflect on how much value you personally place on the item. Ask yourself the following questions to decide if the item in question is something you want to continue to value and keep or if you are comfortable letting it go?

EMOTIONAL VALUE

- What was my original intention for this item?
- How do I use, display, enjoy, or preserve this item currently?
- What factors have contributed to me keeping this item in my possession?
- What are the personal connections, emotional ties, or memories connected to this object?
- If money were not a factor, would I keep this item?
- Is this object valuable to only me?

REAL ESTATE VALUE

- Do I have the space to display or store this item?
- Is the physical space that this object occupies logical and appropriate for this item?
- Does the space where the item is located function well?

- Is my valuable item able to be appreciated or enjoyed in the physical space it is occupying?
- Am I displaying or storing the valuable item to ensure the integrity and value is preserved or maintained?
- Using the formula from Chapter 2, what is the cost per square foot to display or store the item in my space?
- How long, months or years, am I willing to utilize my physical real estate to display or store this valuable object?

MONETARY VALUE

- Do I think my item has monetary value in the market?
- Am I willing to invest in materials or measures needed to appropriately store and preserve this valued object?
- Where can I obtain an honest appraisal for my item?
- What price am I willing to accept to part with this item?
- Is the market value of this object comparable to the money I have spent to store and preserve this item?
- What is the financial investment I am willing to continue in order to keep this object in my possession?
- If the market value appraisal I receive is less than desired, will I feel comfortable to use or enjoy this item? Or will I choose to sell, donate, or continue to store this item?

To begin your journey to realizing the market value or appraisal value for your valued items, search for reputable appraisers and collectors. Google search is a simple first step in researching your valued object. You can review photos, and learn more about the history of an item. eBay is a useful website and marketplace to find similar items being sold. Comparing your items to other items on eBay, can help you to find an honest and realistic value.

If you choose to keep your valued items, ensure that you will use and enjoy them. Instead of waiting for a special occasion to display or use your items, choose to make more days special. Bring out your grandmother's China for Sunday dinners. Use the handmade quilt that was gifted to you during cool winter evenings. Allow your kids to play with your childhood toys so that the joy of these items can continue into the next generation.

When you value items that have an expiration date, give yourself permission to use the valued item before it is unusable. For example, choose to use the expensive perfume and wear it for a date night with your partner. Finding simple moments to enjoy the items you love and cherish will allow you to make more days special. Create a system to help you organize and keep up with product expiration dates. Label each item with the expiration date as a visual reminder to use these special products. Review your products regularly and use them before they expire.

Some items in your possession are valuable to you alone. Reframing your personal connection to your valued objects can help you assess what is most important. Reflect on the value you place on each item in your current chapter of life. The decision to keep or discard the items is the responsibility of you alone. Reframe and R.E.C.L.A.I.M. your space one closet or drawer at a time to create a home environment that you value and enjoy.

If "It has value" strikes a chord with you and you are ready to take action in your space, reference the Tips for Your Personal Reframe & R.E.C.L.A.I.M. Process at the end of our book. Reference the guides at the end of this book: "Resources for Selling Your Unwanted Items" and "Resources for Donating Your Unwanted Items." These guides provide information for next steps for anyone that has reframed their attachment with an item.

CHAPTER 6

IT WAS A GIFT

*"I love giving gifts and I love receiving them.
I really like giving little kids extravagant gifts.
You see their little faces light up and they get excited.
If it's a really good gift, I love receiving it,
like jewels, small islands."*
– Gina Gershon

Jennifer

As a child, my parents tasked me to go through and declutter my toys I no longer played with once or twice a year. I can remember, even at a young age, finding an item I no longer wanted and attempting to place it in a donation pile. But when my mother found a toy that someone had gifted to me, she would stop me and say, "But so-and-so gave that to you. You can't get rid of it." The life lesson I learned as a child was to keep all things that were gifted to me. While my mother's intentions were not to shame me for my decision, feelings of guilt lived with me for decades. As a child I didn't want to disappoint anyone, let alone someone who was kind enough to buy me a gift. Logically, I know this level of guilt is absurd but emotionally I am stuck in this pattern.

Prior to these interactions with my mother, I saw items as what they were, items to be used. If I was not using something I believed I should get rid of it. Now, as an adult, there is an extra layer of guilt I associate with things that are gifted to me, and I continue to struggle with the decision to let go of items or keep them. I store these objects in a box in my garage just in case anyone asks about the item. Has anyone ever asked me about an item they gifted me over five years ago? *No.* Is the item serving a purpose beyond making me feel guilty? *No.* If I gifted someone something and they discarded it, would I want them to feel guilty? *No.* But I hold myself to standards I do not hold others to because I do not want to disappoint anyone.

In my twenties, a close friend gave me a candle holder as a wedding gift. My friend and I had a very fun and playful relationship in college and would frequently play practical jokes on each other. From stealing items and hiding them around campus, to writing fake secret admirer letters, we were always making each other laugh. So in the spirit of that tradition, she bought me the ugliest candle holder she could find. It was intended to be a funny gag gift and remind me of our playful relationship. I loved and appreciated the joke behind the gift, but what was I going to do with it? It was an obnoxiously large and gaudy monkey dressed up in Victorian style clothing, holding a single taper candle holder. It made me smile and laugh every time I saw it, but no one else understood this underlying joke. It severely clashed with my decor. Because of this, it sat at the back of my closet for years collecting dust. Fortunately or unfortunately, it was knocked off the closet shelf and broken. So the decision to part with the gaudy candle holder was made for me and the indecision of what to do with it is gone.

In retrospect, not only are these guilt-associated items taking up the mental space in my brain and physical space in my home, they are also a financial burden. I have paid to move and store several boxes of items that I just do not know what to do with. Although it has become easier for me to let go of these gifted items, the child in me still feels the guilt of discarding something gifted by someone special.

This has been a challenging reframe that I continue to process. But the more I reflect and truly evaluate the merit of each item, the easier it has been to let go of the items that are no longer serving my current lifestyle. I must continue to remind myself that I can choose to let my guilt have the decision-making power or I can empower myself to make the decision to let go of unused or unwanted objects. I know that the gift giver would not want me to keep the item out of guilt or obligation, so I should give myself the same consideration. As I allow others to freely let go of gifts I have bestowed upon them, I am attempting to lift the burden of guilt I place on myself and to choose what items deserve the limited space in my home.

I realized I was also giving gifts out of obligation because I was taught to be polite and bring a gift, so I was perceived as being nice and thoughtful. Although the gifts I gave may not have been wanted by the receiver, I was taught that it is the thought that counts. However, is it truly only the thought that counts or am I unintentionally passing on guilt to someone else that may struggle with this same excuse I have for so many years?

In the past, I purchased souvenirs and gifts that reminded me of someone so I would always have a gift on hand. A storage bin at the top of my closet became my own personal store for gifts and last minute presents just in case I needed one. However, there have been times I have forgotten about the item I purchased for a loved one or the person no longer needed or liked the gift I had previously purchased. By this point it was too late to return the item. The money and time I spent was wasted on a gift that was no longer wanted or needed.

As I have gotten older and my friends and family have become more financially secure, the less I feel obligated to give gifts. We are more able to buy the items that we truly want or need. Because of this, we now celebrate birthdays and holidays with dinners, experiences, and the gift of spending time together. I feel less pressure to purchase items for my loved ones and am learning to reframe how I spend my time and money to show care and love toward others.

REFRAME

"Love the giver more than the gift."
– Brigham Young

Courtney

Most everyone is grateful for gifts from others. Gifts are one way to show someone that you care about them. By taking time to think about someone, and finding something that another person may enjoy or value is a beautiful and loving gesture. However, gifts hold different values to the giver and the receiver. Thirty-two percent of people receive at least one unwanted gift annually according to Gitnux Marketdata Report in 2024. Not all gifts that you receive are meant for you to keep forever. Emotions of sentiment, guilt, and love swirl with the mindset of keeping all gifts that you have been given. Allowing an object to stay in your possession only because it was a gift can create physical clutter in your home's real estate and emotional overwhelm for you personally.

Many people feel stuck without a discerning direction to follow with the gift giving and keeping mindset. We do not want to offend the gift givers nor do we want to seem ungrateful for the gifts others give to us. Remember the stereotypical situation where Grandma gifts the grandchildren socks is a classic gift receiving conundrum. Parents coach their children to smile and say, "Thank you!" to show gratitude for the simple but necessary gift of socks. Although the socks are given with love and affection, the children may not want to offend their grandmother. Another gift giver may present you with a decorative item that does not fit the aesthetic of your home decor. Do you refuse to accept the item or resentfully and begrudgingly place the gifted item in your home? Does the item get stored away with the other items that you have not decided what to do with yet? Keeping and storing items away because of guilt or felt obligation so that feelings are not hurt or someone does not feel disrespected, is not the only choice.

Some gifts do not hold the same value for the recipient, and this is where reframing your mindset surrounding gifts begins. In many people's minds, Aunt Polly would be devastated if you discard this item... Grandfather Jack would be disappointed that you did not keep and display his gift. These feelings of guilt and responsibility can keep you weighed down and stuck. So what do we do when someone we truly love and respect gives us something that is not what we truly want or need? Do we keep the item in closet purgatory or hide it in the garage to collect dust until the end of time? Are you holding onto and keeping each gift because of others' perspectives, feelings, and wants?

Reframing your mindset surrounding gift receiving can help individuals make healthy and more confident decisions about their space and their relationship with things. Lifting the heavy burden of holding onto and keeping each gift because of others' perspectives, feelings, and wants is a challenge for many people. It is important that your wants and needs are also considered in this situation. By focusing and exploring your own feelings and desires about a gift, you can appropriately evaluate each item and consider if this item remains in your current life chapter. This is not a selfish act; this is an honest process for you to reframe and evaluate what is best for you. Helpful reframing can bring you a step closer to less clutter and more space in your real estate.

Below are some helpful reflection and reframing questions to start on your journey to reclaim your space and peace of mind.

REFRAMING QUESTIONS

1. If this object were not in my possession, would I still remember the memories of this time, person, or place?
2. How would I honor and recall the important moments or people associated with this item if this item were not in my possession?
3. Is this object something I hold sentimental value in? Or does this object hold more sentimental value to someone else?
4. If the sentimental value is due to someone one else valuing this object, why do I feel obligated to keep this item? Is this felt obligation something I would expect of someone else?

5. Can anyone else find value or purpose in this item besides me? If so, could this object be more useful for someone else in their possession?
6. How would I feel knowing the object would be used more often than I am currently using it? Would that make a difference?
7. How much sentimental value does this object really hold if I do not choose to display this item in my home's real estate?

* * * * *

R.E.C.L.A.I.M. Case Study

It Was A Gift

The client for this chapter is reviewing and evaluating artwork from her home. Most of the artwork has been gifted or inherited to her or her husband from family members. She explains that the artwork is appreciated, but, the artwork is not displayed and does not match their home aesthetic. She has held onto these pieces of artwork because she does not want to offend those who gifted the art. The artwork has continued to be stored and not displayed as they have relocated from one state to another and moved from house to house over the years. Currently, it is stacked up in her garage or hidden behind furniture in her bedroom.

Before we started the Reframe and R.E.C.L.A.I.M. process, we asked a few questions to better understand the client and her perspectives.

What have been the obstacles for you in assessing and evaluating the items you want to address today?
The whole stack of pictures/paintings feels overwhelming. I thought it would take forever to go through, and it hasn't been the highest priority item on my list, so I keep procrastinating.

How long have you been accumulating the items we will be reviewing today?
Almost twenty years.

How do you feel when you see this space today?
Ready for a change. It seems so obvious that it needs to be done now that we are totally focused on it today. It's embarrassing that it has taken so long to address.

Is there anything about this process that you think may be uncomfortable for you?
Making decisions. I'm very indecisive and sentimental. It reminds me of another unfinished project, and it gives me anxiety.

As we start the R.E.C.L.A.I.M. process, we will go through the seven-step process below:

R – REFLECT on the current space.

The pile of artwork we are reviewing is leaning up against the middle of her bedroom wall under the window in a very visually prominent space. This prominent location adds to the client's anxiety.

How is this space currently being used?
Storage. It's right in the walkway and I'm afraid someone will trip over the artwork or break a piece. It needs to be moved.

How do you hope to feel when you see this space once the Reframe & Reclaim process is complete?
Closure. I think I will feel much calmer walking into the space and enjoy it more. The pile of items is always in view reminding me that I need to take care of it. Placing the artwork on the walls to be displayed is the last step to finish this room.

What's given you the inspiration to start this today?
The piles of art have been moved four times now, from home to home. There is a box of art in the garage that has not been gone through since we moved into this house and was probably still in the box when we previously moved the time before that. So it's probably been in a box for about nine years. It's a visual representation of my procrastination. It's easier to go along with delaying the process when the furniture isn't set but now it's time. The furniture feels like it flows well so now it's time to say goodbye to the pieces of art that don't work anymore. Some of the pieces bring me pain when I see them because they remind me of past chapters of my life. The pieces I really like are not being hung up and enjoyed. I need that closure to move forward.

E – EVALUATE each item and understand the true value each item has for you as you empty the space. Reimagine how this space functions.

As we began to evaluate the artwork she had in her home, we started with the pieces that the client had already contemplated letting go. Then we moved on to the more emotionally challenging art pieces that were gifted. As we began to sift through the different pieces of artwork, she shared stories of loved ones who gave the gifts and the reasons the art was so special for her.

Tell me about this piece of artwork with the painted magnolias.
This piece was painted by my husband's great-grandmother and was gifted to him. It always hung in his grandmother's house, and she has since passed. I love magnolias and this piece. It needs to find a place where it can be seen and enjoyed more.

Other pieces brought negative memories and emotions. Some were related to family and others were related to a previous career that was no longer being pursued by the client.

I can tell you are having some feelings about this map. What memories do you have connected to this artwork?
My career was as a geologist. This map was a gift from an intern I worked with. It's reprinted from a hand drawn topographic map from 1915. It was hanging in my office. When I look at it, It makes me sad because I was laid-off from that job. It was a very negative experience. It's a cool piece but it doesn't go with my decor anymore. I have other items to remind me of geology that make me feel good. It needs to move on as I have. My previous career and these pieces don't define me anymore. I have other priorities.

The piece is added to the donation pile. We move on to another piece of art that was a gift from her husband's family.

Client: This was a gift from an uncle and aunt who are no longer together. It used to make me feel uncomfortable and bring up the bad memories surrounding their divorce. It's been long enough that I can enjoy it as the piece of art it is. They did not have children so it was passed to my husband. I love that it is serene and I love the colors and impressionist art style. I think I had to live with it for a while and it had to become "our art." Not the art from our aunt and uncle.

One item that is considered is a calligraphy scripture that belonged to her husband's deceased grandfather.

Tell me about this artwork and is there any sentimental value or memory tied to this gift?
My husband loves this piece. It had been hanging in his office in our previous home, but I've kept it safe in bubble wrap until we find a proper place to hang it in our current home.

As we are evaluating the artwork in her bedroom, the client's husband walks in to see the progress being made.

Client: Hey, where do you want to hang this piece?
Client's Husband: What piece?
Client: The scripture from your grandfather's job when he retired.
Client's Husband: Oh, is that what it was from? It doesn't matter to me where we hang it. I don't care about it that much.

It surprises the client to hear her husband has no attachment to the artwork. All of the years she has made it a priority to carefully store and preserve this family artwork to only realize that her husband does not value this artwork as she assumed he did.

Client: Oh, the lies we tell ourselves. Here I had it in my mind it was super-sentimental. Well, that's another thing to get rid of.

Once all of the artwork has been examined, the client is able to identify the pieces that hold positive feelings and remind her of fond memories. She is able to let go of the pieces of artwork that do not fit her current chapter of life and release negative memories that have kept her stuck in procrastination. Next, we begin to evaluate each item's aesthetic value and where each piece of artwork may fit into her home's decor.

C – CLEAN the space. Empty and clean the space so that it feels like a fresh, clean slate.

How do you feel seeing this space empty versus how you felt with the space occupied with items?
I feel relieved. The items have been processed and a decision has been made. That's the big thing. It's not this weight anymore. The wall and floor of my bedroom are empty so I feel good. I feel there's been progress.

L – LAYOUT and label the space before placing any items back into the space. Attempt to create a blueprint of how the space will look and feel. Measure and readjust the space to fit the space's new functionality, as well as any organizational materials that you may include to enhance the aesthetic and functionality.

After the Evaluation process, we reviewed all of the art that was staying in the client's home. The client was redesigning her home's family gallery wall in the entry hallway of the home. We brainstormed several ideas and the client decided to reimagine her display space by incorporating the artwork created by family members into her gallery wall.

An arched alcove in the front hallway of their home is a prominent place that all visitors view as they walk into the front door of the home. The bottom of the alcove serves as a display shelf where the client stores her family photo albums and framed photos.

The next step in the R.E.C.L.A.I.M. process is to begin to lay out how the space will function and be viewed. Using painter's tape, we measure and tape out a space on her floor to visualize the space. Being mindful of the alcove and the curvature of the space, we also measured and taped out the varying heights and locations of the photo albums, tabletop frames, and candle holders that will occupy the space to ensure that the wall art will fully be visible once all of the furnishings and decor have been added.

We begin by laying out the artwork and family photos to best utilize the wall space and create a cohesive and aesthetically pleasing design. However, after the initial layout of the family gallery, the client is not satisfied.

Client: I don't know if this is what I want. I've been looking forward to hanging the pictures and art but now, it's not feeling right.

Upon further reflection, the client reveals that family dynamics have shifted recently. Seeing two of the family photos that were previously in this space now brings sadness for the client. The client decides to remove these negatively charged photographs and add different photographs of her nieces and nephews that evoke a happier feeling. The client is continuing to reframe and reclaim this space as she evaluates which objects now belong and what pieces of art no longer serve the function she desires for her family gallery wall. We continue to move artwork and photographs in the measured area until everything feels balanced with representation of both the maternal and paternal family lineage.

A – ASSEMBLE items back into the space and adjust as needed. Allow for trial and error as you reimagine the space's blueprint. This may be adjusting materials, changing where items are located, or reframing what items are truly intended for this new environment.

Using the wall layout that is measured and taped on the floor we are able to quickly and easily transfer the pictures and artwork onto the alcove wall. We relocate two 8" x 10" pictures with her son's school photos. These photos were previously displayed on the alcove shelf and took up a large amount of real estate in this space. Now they are hung above each of her son's backpacks creating a personalized school drop zone. The photos are hanging low enough that the kids can easily see them and identify where to hang their backpacks and the client can update the photos each year.

We also take this time to hang a few other additional pieces throughout her home, continuing to reclaim the different spaces and creating a more functional and aesthetically pleasing home environment. The magnolia painting found in the client's pile of artwork was hung in the living room where it will be seen and enjoyed daily by the entire family. Now instead of being hidden in a box or stored behind furniture, these paintings and family memories can now find new life and bring joy to the entire family every day

I – INSPECT the space once everything is reassembled. Step back and take inventory, viewing the aesthetic and functionality of the newly reimagined space. This is the final gut check.

Does this space now match the intention you imagined?

Yes. It was supposed to be a space that highlighted our family and what we stand for and now it does that. Incorporating family artwork into the family gallery wall was a great idea. It's not overwhelming, it fits the space and I don't think I could have put it together myself. It looks complete, like it's supposed to look.

Does this space now fit your space's function and your current lifestyle needs?

Yes. Now everything is put together, it's organized and it's finished where it wasn't before. It's satisfying to have everything organized and have culled through and edited out some of the pictures. It feels more cohesive and better this way because we're not forcing the pieces in. I liked that we used the art instead of only pictures hanging on the family gallery wall. Specifically with the gallery wall it was a big blank space that wanted to be used. It was a constant reminder that it needed to be done. Now the picture frames on the alcove shelf and the table look like it's on purpose instead of having the table covered in picture frames. It was messy before.

REFRAME & RECLAIM

AFTER

M – MAINTAIN your space. Remember that this space will only stay as organized and aesthetically pleasing as you put effort and intentionality into it. Create a plan and a system to purposefully maintain this new space, recruiting any other people needed that utilize or enjoy this space. Accountability is key.

As we neared the end of the seven-step R.E.C.L.A.I.M. process with this client, we wanted to ensure that our client had awareness and a plan of action to continue to maintain this beautiful space she had helped to create for her home.

What system will you put in place to keep this space as you see it today?

I will decide on one piece at a time and not let them pile up. I will take a picture of it, as suggested, if I want to keep a reminder before letting go of something.

What steps will you need to take to assure that this space will continue to function and feel like it does right now?

For the family gallery wall space, I won't let the table get covered. Keep it as clean as possible so it will continue to look like a finished space. I will update some of the photos as my kids grow but those pictures are on the table and easy to access. The ones hanging on the wall won't be changed and that's great because I won't have to think about them.

We also want to evaluate how our client experienced the seven steps of R.E.C.L.A.I.M. We asked her the following questions:

How did you feel during the process?

Good. Calm, focused, not rushed. So excited. I feel relieved to have someone help me finish this.

Was the R.E.C.L.A.I.M. process what you expected it to be?
It was so much faster. I think it really helped to talk through the pieces, honoring them, giving them their moment and then I was more able to let them go. It was hugely helpful for me not to have to touch the items, as that would make me want to decide later.

It's weird because you think it's going to be scary or extra painful and it's not so bad. Then you think, *Why did I take so long to go through the items?* You think about each item, you validate what you're feeling, and now I know I'm keeping a piece for a reason. We got through the art in two hours and if I were to go through it myself, it would have taken much longer. It would have been too painful to give it the mental space it deserves and I would continue to procrastinate. I'm very indecisive and I let my anxiety and "protective procrastination" keep me from tackling the project. It's too much pressure when I'm the only one thinking in my head. It helps to validate feelings and not feel pressure with someone else I know in the room. Reflection can sometimes be difficult but it's an important thing, and I can move forward with clarity. I'm glad that I can identify what's important and get rid of the rest. By doing the process, I was able to confidently validate what I'm keeping and not keeping and verify memories of what I thought was sentimental and what wasn't.

Do you feel comfortable to continue this process now that you have experienced it today?
I do. This was definitely a confidence-building exercise for me. I am capable of making difficult choices and moving forward. I know that I will feel so much better when I am done. I feel energized because now I know the value of the pieces I enjoy and I want them to be up on the walls. I'm ready to hang things where they can be seen. It feels right. Hanging the family-created artwork together was an idea I was missing that I didn't know I needed.

What space do you hope to evaluate next?
My master closet. It's going to be a big job, but I can break it into smaller tasks and make steady progress.

What advice do you have for others that are unsure about starting or just beginning this process?
I personally thought it was so helpful to work through the process with someone you trust. If you have a friend or family member that already knows your story, your heart and even your obstacles, they can help you make difficult decisions. Be brave, take that first step. And if you feel overwhelmed or need to walk away for a minute, go ahead. But come back and persevere, keep trudging up that switchback. The view from the top is totally worth it.

Is there anything about the process you would change?
No, I think it was great. I love the questions. They help you realize why you have been putting it off and move forward. Thank you.

Any feedback you have for us as we have helped you facilitate this process?
I think making a day of it relieved some of the anxiety.

FOLLOW-UP

Three months later, we follow-up with the client and reflect back on the R.E.C.L.A.I.M. process to evaluate if it is still working for her. The client previously admitted that she is not decisive and easily second guesses herself. We wonder if she has continued to make decisions with confidence about her home and her belongings.

Now that you've lived with the system for a few months how does it feel?

It feels really good. Instead of the artwork being stacked in a pile where it is not being used it is now out where my family can enjoy it.

Does it still work? Anything you would change?

Once we lived with the artwork for a while, we realized the Magnolia painting that hung where we could all see and enjoy it was constantly being touched by our son when he was in time-out. We did not want to move the painting as we loved it hanging where it was, so we moved the time-out space instead. The new time-out space is working well and we can still enjoy the Magnolia painting we love so much and reminds us of our loved one.

There was also a piece that originally hung in the kitchen but the wall it previously hung on was covered with a new storage cabinet. I really wanted to see the painting more often and hang it in a more prominent spot. After reflecting on the process, I realized the artwork I was hanging in my bathroom was not my favorite and was taking up wall space. It had been there so long it became like wallpaper and I didn't even notice it anymore. So I replaced it with the piece from the kitchen I really loved and now it pops out at me so I notice it daily. The new piece is very soothing and calming, which is more the aesthetic I was going for. It just makes me smile.

Do you have any regrets about letting go of any of your items?

No. It's a relief not having to think about the task of going through the artwork. It is taken care of and done, and I don't have to worry about it anymore. It felt like it was going to take longer and be more emotionally draining because I had to make decisions about each piece. I was anticipating a lot of decision fatigue and the process helped simplify and make it easier. It's a big relief to not be wondering about that pile and what I'm missing out on. The pieces I gave away are out of sight, out of mind. I know I'm using the pieces I love and I'm not just storing them.

How has this process helped you to reframe your relationship with your things?
I will definitely be more mindful in the future about new pieces I purchase. If I do buy a new piece I would have to decide where it would hang and its aesthetic before I bring it into my home.

Have you started to evaluate any other spaces in your home since your first R.E.C.L.A.I.M. process with us?
Yes. All my spaces. It's changed my perspective as to how and what process I would use to make decisions. I think my main resistance before was the emotional drain and decision fatigue. I am a very indecisive person and tend to overthink things. Now that I know I can trust the process I'm not so worried.

* * * *

For Your Personal R.E.C.L.A.I.M. Process

Just as seasons of life change and your feelings toward objects change, the items in your home may need to be reevaluated. Each chapter of life brings new changes and possible challenges. Your family and your partner's perspectives and feelings will change as well. Checking in periodically and evaluating your space, the items in your space and your feelings about the items in your space is helpful. Ensuring that the objects that you keep in your real estate hold the same value as previous chapters can be a helpful strategy to ensure that your belongings and gifts continue to be valued in your home.

Start with your personal experience with a gift. Reflect and ask yourself the questions below:

- How did I feel when I received the gift?
- How do I feel now about the gift?
- Is the gift serving a purpose?
- Is the gift on display?

If the reflections to the questions above are mostly positive and you want to keep the gift, how can you honor it and allow it to be more purposeful in your space? Is there an appropriate place for this gift to be displayed or used? How can this gift become a more prominent part of your home and your space?

However, if your reflections are mostly negative toward the gift, it may be time to let go of the gift and begin to reclaim your space. Start by placing the undesired gifts in a container and store it in another room. If you feel comfortable after some time, you can begin to donate or discard the gifts that you do not desire in your space.

If your goal is to reduce the clutter in your space, and you have generous friends and family members that enjoy giving, it can be challenging to have conversations surrounding gifts. However, having these crucial conversations, sooner rather than later, will reduce the feelings of guilt for yourself and allow you to recruit others to support your ultimate goals. People cannot read minds, and if you do not communicate your intentions for your home, others will unknowingly be counterproductive to your goals. Open and honest communication is helpful for any relationship. Lack of communication about your wants, needs, and goals for your home and lifestyle can create conflict, confusion, and frustration for everyone involved.

If you think someone may guilt you into keeping a gift, having a conversation with them about your personal feelings and perspectives can allow the other party to better understand you and your wants and needs. Ultimately, you do not need permission to let go of a gift that was given to you if it is not serving you or your lifestyle. Offering to return the gift to the giver is a first step option in this situation. This does not discount the gratitude or appreciation you may have for the sentiment of the gift, but it does allow the giver to better understand you. This is also a gesture in offering back to the giver something that they may have valued or spent time or money on and allow the giver to feel appreciated even if the gift is not appreciated specifically.

Another option, if you are unsure how the gift giver may respond to you offering to return the gift to the giver, is to simply tell them that you no longer want or need the gift and have decided to donate it to someone who may appreciate it more in their current life chapter. This step allows the gift to continue to have value but also allows the gift to be appreciated in someone else's space and not continue to take up your valuable real estate.

Reflecting on the enjoyment of the item, the value, and how the item fits into your home aesthetic and your personal lifestyle chapter is helpful in deciding if you keep, donate, or discard something that has been gifted to you. Ultimately, the decisions that you make about your home and your space is *your* decision. You and your household are the ones that have the consequences for your home's comfort, function, and lifestyle. You have the power to make decisions for yourself and create an environment in your space that best serves you and your household.

Below are other strategies and options for you and the gifts you have received.

- Take photographs of the gift and give it away. You can still reference the photo of the item to remember, but it will not be taking up the physical space in your home. This can be especially helpful with items that take up large amounts of space. Include a small written card with each item in the photograph that encapsulates important information to keep record if desired.
- Would another family member appreciate or enjoy the gift and have the desire and space to use it or display it?
- If an organization or individual can use the gift, would it be a better manner in which to honor the item?
- For the gifts that bring pain and heartache, those bring their own set of mental and emotional challenges to address. We will discuss these items in Chapter 10 in more detail.

Along with receiving a gift, there is also the perspective of the gift giver. Approximately thirty percent of Americans shop throughout the year for holiday gifts according to Gitnux Marketdata Report in 2024. Some givers are very generous and choose to store excessive amounts of gifts in the event that a gift is needed for an occasion. Always having a gift to give helps them to feel gracious and thoughtful; however, giving a gift just for giving's sake leads to an obligation to the receiver to accept a gift that may not be desired. Giving a gift to someone is a kind act when the gift is given with authenticity. Knowing your gift recipient and their lifestyle allows the giver to give more appreciated and valued gifts. Before giving a gift, take the time to reflect on the person receiving the gift and what they value.

Continuously collecting items to give is a "Catch 22" for some. Feeling compelled to give to others can help a gift giver feel helpful, needed, and serve a purpose. These attributes are honorable, of course; however, collecting gifts just to give away does need to have some boundaries. Ensuring that the gift giver is not over-giving of their time, money, and resources is imperative for a healthy lifestyle. When reframing your habits surrounding gift giving, keep in mind that fifty-six percent of people prefer to give and receive experiences as gifts rather than material items (Gitnux Marketdata Report in 2024).

Tangible gifts are only one way to share love and appreciation for others. Below are a few alternative experiential gift ideas to consider.

- Memberships to museums or favorite places
- Gift cards to a favorite restaurant
- Tickets to an event or concert
- Cook a meal for someone
- Deliver favorite food items
- Host a dinner party
- Host a game night
- Babysit kids so parents can have a night out
- Plants for a home or office
- Activity for friends or family to do together (painting, pottery, roller-skating, picnic, hike, bike riding, etc.)
- Money toward an upcoming vacation
- Gas cards for new drivers
- Subscription based activities
- Charitable donations in honor of someone

If "It was a gift" strikes a chord with you and you are ready to take action in your space, reference the Tips for Your Personal Reframe & R.E.C.L.A.I.M. Process at the end of our book.

CHAPTER 7

IT'S SENTIMENTAL

*"I'm holding onto my kids' art projects and report cards
so that one day, many years from now,
she will spend three seconds barely looking at them
before tossing them all in the garbage."*
– Anonymous

Jennifer

Death has almost always been a constant in my life. When I was nine, both of my grandfathers passed away. My dad died when I was fifteen. My uncle and both grandmothers died when I was twenty-five. At a young age I learned how to evaluate what my loved ones left behind by the examples of the adults in my life. I witnessed the adults in my life expressing an array of emotions connected with items of deceased loved ones. Emotions ranged from tear-filled smiles as an object conjured a happy memory, laughter at ridiculous items of clothing someone loved, and guilt associated with items that reminded my family members of unfinished dreams of those who passed.

When my maternal grandfather passed away, the adults in my family allowed my brother, cousins, and I the opportunity to take a few of his knick-knacks "to remember him by." Because of this, I have almost always had this mentality that items are tied to memories, and vice versa. I did not get a chance to know either of my grandfathers well. They did not live nearby, so I only saw each of them a couple of times a year at most. I was also nine years old and did not have the life skills to build meaningful and reciprocal relationships. For example, even as a young child I knew a ceramic miniature dachshund did not significantly relate to my grandfather's lifestyle, but, it was something from his home that I liked. Therefore, this was the item I chose to connect with him after he died. I proudly displayed the dachshund in my room to give me a glimpse of the small part of his life that I knew. Considering the emotional value I placed on the dachshund from the very little I knew of my grandfather, you can only imagine the sentimental stronghold in which I embraced any item related to my father. He died suddenly when I was fifteen years old.

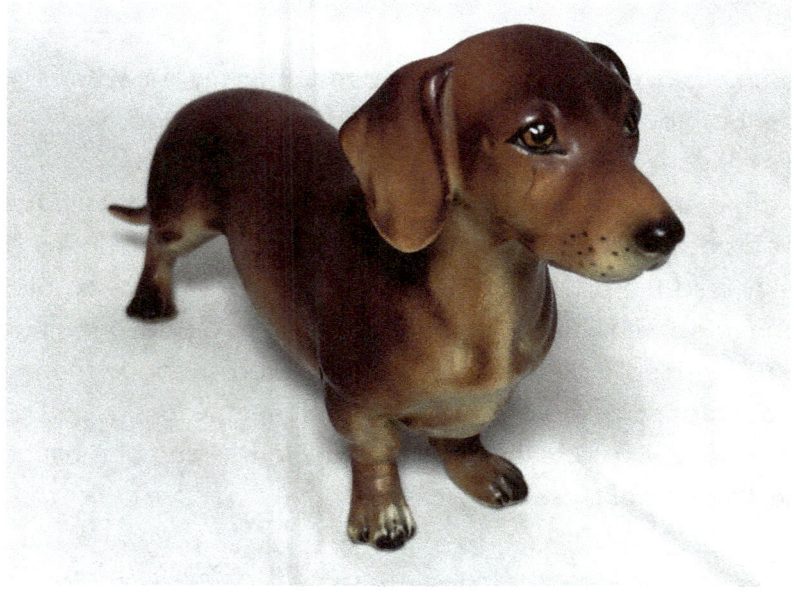

To add to the complexity, I now realize that I was trying to keep all the items that were related to good memories as my father and I did not have the best relationship toward the end of his life. I was a teenage girl and he was... well, to be honest, I did not really know who he was. Again, at this age in life, I did not have the life experience and maturity to really see him, or my mother, as fully independent people with separate identities outside of being my parents. My dad was active in my life, attending sporting events, encouraging me to do my best in school, and being a typical parent. However, as most teenagers are, I was more focused on myself than others. I was stuck in this attempt to connect with my father and found the only way I knew how was to hold onto any object that tied me to the memories I had with him.

I can remember in my early twenties beginning to forget small details of the memories of my father. To me, it felt like forgetting my memories of my father was like forgetting him. The fear of forgetting was haunting me. How could someone who had such an influential impact on my life so easily drift from my memory? In retrospect, I should have been more forgiving of myself considering that at twenty years old I had already lived a quarter of my life without him. Today, if I try to remember details of the last quarter of my life, I do not expect to remember everything.

A therapist once told me that it was normal for individuals to forget some memories made with loved ones. It is impossible to remember each minute of every day. Our brains do not have the capacity to hold on to all of the information we encounter every day. However, as people continue to spend time with their loved ones, they are constantly creating new memories. When new memories cannot be created with loved ones who have passed, we strive to retain the few memories we have. Some do this by keeping items that trigger memories of their loved one.

At the time, my fear-based thinking had me stuck, collecting any item that I could tie to my father and fearing that I could not discard any item because I would also discard memories and a connection with him. I questioned if I would have memories to share with my children, his grandchildren that he will never meet. I struggled to believe that the items I kept would be enough to remember him.

Today, I still have several of my father's shirts that I have held onto through the years. They are shirts that I did not like when he was living but I am so fearful of losing the memory of him that I continue to keep them. I keep the cologne he wore so I can remember his smell. I keep my 16" x 20" freshman JV high school basketball team photo because he was so proud that I made the team. Basketball was one thing my dad strongly bonded over. Do I have it hanging on the wall? No. Did I EVER have it hanging on the wall? No. So why is the guilt and fear of discarding these items so strong? Intellectually, I know that my father would not be mad at me if I let go of these items. I also understand that these items will not guarantee that I will retain the memory associated with my dad.

Thinking of all of the items I have held onto so tightly for the past twenty-five years, I question if moving and storing the boxes from place to place has done more harm than good? When was the last time I opened those boxes? The overflow of stuff that consumes my garage today causes me stress every time I walk into the space. The stress of moving is compounded because I have extra boxes of sentimental items I must continue to move and store. I am not quite sure what is in each of the boxes, but if I REALLY valued these items would they be stored in a box out in my garage for all of these years? Or am I only repeating the habits I grew up learning from the adults in my family? The generational patterns were continuing with me and my home. My garage was beginning to resemble the basement of my grandfather.

REFRAME

*"Too much sentiment and no reason,
destroys both the path and the pedestrian."*
– Abhijit Naskar, *Giants in Jeans: 100 Sonnets of United Earth*

Courtney

It is in our human nature to strive for connection. It is literally innately wired in our DNA to connect with others. We are social beings and need a sense of community. However, when the connection cannot be made in our daily reality, objects can become a surrogate to our feeling of security and belonging. This is apparent when the death of a loved one occurs. The need to connect physically with that person cannot be fulfilled; therefore, holding on to objects that remind us of that person creates a feeling of continued connection and bond to that person. The sentiment of possessing an item to gain a sense of connection or validation happens to us all in some way.

What is sentiment? According to *Merriam Webster*, sentiment is a romanticized or nostalgic feeling that is brought up in a person. How do we ignite this sentimentality? Tangible objects, items we can see and touch, do this well. This is one of the reasons so many humans are challenged with the idea to part with or discard an item that brings warm and comforting memories.

Many objects can trigger a fond memory of a time, person or place. Sometimes, the emotional attachment to objects can be very strong, creating a challenge to separate oneself with the thing that sends our mind into a past chapter of our lives. When we get hung up on the idea that I cannot part with this ball cap because it reminds me of the first baseball game my father took me to, we must also consider if it is the object that holds the memory or if we can still recall and revisit those memories without the objects we keep? If I part with this frayed ball cap, will my memories of this time fray as well?

We must differentiate the process of sentimental collection versus *sentimental recollection*. Realizing that the collection of memories is not measured by the collection of things we hold in our possession is a first step in finding a healthy balance of sentimentality. And if every item we possess seems to strike a sentimental chord, this becomes all the more difficult to filter through the things that bring memories to mind and realizing that those memories can still be held and recalled without holding onto each and every item.

There is nothing unhealthy or morally wrong with being a person that is struck by sentiment; however, an unbalanced collection of sentimentality can have a negative effect on our mental health, physical health, and overall well-being. When people express unusually strong attachments to objects, places, events, and beliefs, this can create an unhealthy stuckness and attachment to our possessions. Sadly, the intention of holding onto things for purely sentimental purposes can quickly build a stock pile of clutter, disorganization, and mental overwhelm and stress.

When does sentiment turn unhealthy and possibly harmful? When intrusive thoughts begin to disrupt your life or compulsive actions disallow someone to live a healthy functioning life, sentimentality becomes a dysfunction. Creating an unhealthy bond to possessions can also develop into an unhealthy and false sense of security. The belief that the more items I have in my possession guarantees a more secure connection to someone or something, is a distorted belief. People recall memories in many different ways.

Storytelling, photographs, and traditions are all different avenues that many people utilize to find a connection and create memories. Understanding your purpose in holding onto an item that brings memories and sentimental value is an important step in self-awareness. What are the reasons, justifications, or excuses you tell yourself in holding onto items that strike a sentimental chord for you?

The reason for our sentiment is an important topic. What do I gain or receive by keeping, displaying, storing, and carrying this object with me through life? Does it bring me contentment, spark a fond memory? Does the thought of not having this item create anxiety, fear, worry or guilt? Do I hold onto this object out of a felt obligation? Do you feel as though you may become incomplete without this item? Do you feel that you will feel insecure or not feel safe without this item?

Bottom line: Is the reason I keep this item more helpful or harmful for me today? Is holding on to this thing bringing me peace and joy or is it bringing me stress, guilt, worry, or anxiety?

So, how do we REFRAME our ideas of sentimental recollection and RECLAIM our physical and mental real estate? Sentimental value is held in the eye of the beholder. What is valuable to me, may not be sentimentally valuable to another. REFRAMING our mindset surrounding physical objects and their sentimental value is very challenging. Here are a few questions to ask yourself as you are reevaluating what holds the most sentimental value to you.

REFRAMING QUESTIONS

1. If this object were not in my possession, would I still remember the memories of this time, person, or place?
2. How would I honor and recall the important moments or people associated with this item if this item were not in my possession?
3. Is this object something I hold sentimental value in? Or does this object hold more sentimental value to someone else?
4. If the sentimental value is due to someone one else valuing this object, why do I feel obligated to keep this item? Is this felt obligation something I would expect of someone else?
5. Can anyone else find value or purpose in this item besides me? If so, could this object be more useful for someone else in their possession?
6. How would I feel knowing the object would be used more often than I am currently using it? Would that make a difference?
7. How much sentimental value does this object really hold if I do not choose to display this item in my home's real estate?

When you begin to reflect and realize the intention and true understanding of your sentimental grip, you can start the process of reframing what holds the most sentimental value for you. This is NOT what holds value for someone else, NOT keeping objects out of undue obligation, and NOT what you think someone else may want for you. Unclutching the strong grip you hold on each of these items and examining their true value FOR YOU can be insightful, rewarding, and relieving. Remember that this is a process... *your* process. Take the time you need to reflect and explore the reframing questions above to help you determine the true sentimental value of each of your items. The only person making these decisions is *you*.

* * * * *

R.E.C.L.A.I.M. Case Study

It's Sentimental

The client for this chapter inherited many items from several close family members who had passed away throughout the years. Before our session the items were stored in a curio cabinet located inside her home that was visible once you stepped through the front door. It is located in a prominent location, where she proudly displays items of sentiment and family heritage. However, each shelf was overly filled, making it difficult to appreciate any of the items. What was intended to be a beautiful display of valued family heirlooms was distorted to resemble a repurposed glass storage box.

Before we started the Reframe and R.E.C.L.A.I.M. process, we asked a few questions to better understand our client and her perspectives.

What have been the obstacles for you in assessing and evaluating the items you want to address today?

I previously believed If I let go of these things, I would not remember them. I will remember them because they're my parents, but it has taken me a long time to believe that logical side. For example, there are beer steins. I don't drink beer, so is it logical for me to have beer steins from Germany or occupied Japan? It is also partially the fear of getting rid of something that might be valuable.

How long have you been accumulating the items we will be reviewing today?
Probably fifty years.

How do you feel when you see this space today?
There is no organization. Items are just shoved in wherever I can put them. It does not look attractive at all. It's stressful to look at.

How do you feel now with us here to start the Reframe & Reclaim process?
I feel relieved that somebody is going to help me make the decisions in a non-judgmental way. You are here to help, not criticize.

R – REFLECT on the current space.

What is your hope for the functionality of this space?
I hope it is pleasing to the eye and it's not stressful to look at it. It would look good if it was organized and thinned out. I hope to be able to see the individual items in the cabinet instead of a mess of unrelated things.

How do you hope to feel when you see this space once the Reframe & Reclaim process is complete?
I think I'll feel better because I'll have less visual clutter. I've been trying to purge stuff, so it is a good feeling to take a critical look at things and put things where they're supposed to be.

What's given you the inspiration to start this today?
I'm tired of looking at the curio cabinet as it is now because it is junky and chaotic. I want it to look pretty, and I need someone to help me go through and help me make the tough decisions. I don't want to become a hoarder for things that don't matter.

REFRAME & RECLAIM

E – EVALUATE each item and understand the true value each item has for you as you empty the space. Reimagine how this space functions. *How does each item fit into your aspirational space? Does each item match the feel and function you imagined for the space?*

We declutter the space with the client paying special attention to the items gifted to her from her parents. We separate the items that held the most sentimental value to the client from the other items that did not meet the functionality or aesthetic of the space.

As we continue to evaluate each item found in her curio cabinet, we come across several Star Wars and Disney World cups that were stacked together and hidden behind multiple beer steins.

Client: Oh my cups!

What are you thinking about when you see these cups?
I'm thinking of going to Disney World. Of fun times. These are from our first trip to Disney as a family. I had gotten a bonus from work which enabled us to go. I was very excited as I was forty-three, and it was my first trip to Disney. It was also one of the last trips we took with my late husband. He passed away later that year. I have since gone back to Disney several times with my family and have made several fond memories there.

Do you like the cups to be in the curio cabinet stored this way, stacked, or would you like them to be separated and displayed?
They would have to go back in the curio cabinet, but If there is room I would like them to be separated and displayed.

Prioritize and keep what holds the most value. If everything is hidden you can't see the items you truly value.

The client continues to sort through and prioritize what items truly hold sentimental value and warrant a sacred place to be displayed in her curio cabinet. She finds some items to both be sentimental and have usefulness. The useful items were separated from the sentimental items and placed in her home to be used. This included several Boston Celtics glasses commemorating their sixteen championship wins from 1957-1986, which she decided to use as everyday drinking glasses. In the curio cabinet, they were hidden on a lower shelf but now she can use and enjoy them every day. Other items found in her curio cabinet carry a much higher sentimental value and need to be preserved and displayed only. By removing the Celtic glasses, it creates more space for the purely sentimental Disney and Star Wars cups she wanted to preserve. Now they are on display in her curio cabinet to be seen and admired.

As we continue evaluating her items, the client wants to preserve the history of each item. She decides to write on a piece of paper the object's history and significance for her. The client fills out a small card with all the information she found valuable to tell each item's story.

She hopes that the origins and history of the sentimental pieces she has displayed will one day be passed down to her children. At that time, they can decide if the items hold the same value for them or choose to part with the items when they are inherited. If someone else finds the item they will understand the family history and the reason it held value to the owner.

Are you having any hesitations about the items you decided to let go of?
If you have a few things that you can look at and remember your loved one by, I think that's really all you need. And some of the things they bequeathed me I'm never going to use. Like beer steins. I'm not a beer drinker and most of them were decorative but what good are they doing for me? They're just gathering dust.

Now that you see all of the items we have removed from the cabinet, is it hard to imagine all of these items fitting into your curio cabinet?
Yes. The curio cabinet was jammed and unorganized and you could hardly see what was in it. But this way it's a lot better because I can see things that are most important to me. I can see the thing my parents gave me and my late husband's items and remember them very readily. It's not blocked by things I felt obligated to keep.

C – CLEAN the space. Empty and clean the space so that it feels like a fresh, clean slate.

Once the curio cabinet is empty and all items are removed from the space, the shelves are removed and cleaned thoroughly. The client remarks that she has not cleaned the curio cabinet since the display was originally set up. The curio cabinet has new life and a brightness that is much needed. The cabinet now resembles a true treasure chest waiting to be filled with the most sentimental valued items held in the client's possession.

L – LAYOUT and label the space before placing any items back into the space. Attempt to create a blueprint of how the space will look and feel. Measure and readjust the space to fit the space's new functionality, as well as any organizational materials that you may include to enhance the aesthetic and functionality.

Next we use Post-it notes to layout the space. We group like items together to reimagine the categories needed and allocate the appropriate amount space for each identified group. For example, cups occupy one shelf, family heirlooms are displayed on three shelves, and sentimental items from life experiences are placed on two shelves. Then, measuring the items and adjusting shelves, we grouped the categorized items together for a cohesive and aesthetically pleasing display for all of her sentimental collections in the curio cabinet.

A – ASSEMBLE items back into the space and adjust as needed. Allow for trial and error as you reimagine the space's blueprint. This may be adjusting materials, changing where items are located or reframing what items are truly intended for this new environment.

Now that the space is cleared out and clean, it is ready to be filled intentionally. We discuss how the client wants the items to be displayed in the curio cabinet.

What are the most important items that you want to highlight in the most prominent display areas?

Kitchen Items from my grandmother. A green glass butter dish and a gold pitcher and creamer set. I remember the butter dish from my childhood, and it reminds me of what a great cook she was. She made the best homemade rolls and cinnamon rolls. They were fantastic! I was fifteen when she died, and she didn't write down her recipes, so these items are what I have left of her. I was blessed to have sweet and loving grandmothers. The Star Wars and Muppet glasses give me fond memories of my children. They are the glasses they used to drink out of when they were kids.

We continue to place items in the curio cabinet as the client confirms the placement of each item, ensuring that individual items can be clearly seen. Not only is our assembly process focusing on the sentimental value of each kept item, our intention is to create an aesthetically pleasing display for all of her home visitors to enjoy when they walk into her front door.

We also include the small written cards that encapsulate important information about the most sentimental items for the client in the display case. This will allow the client to more easily share stories about each item as well as document the historical and sentimental significance for family members and friends alike. The curio cabinet is now transformed from a dusty and cluttered knick-knack storage unit into a clean and well defined family heirloom.

BEFORE

REFRAME & RECLAIM

I – INSPECT the space once everything is reassembled. Step back and take inventory, viewing the aesthetic and functionality of the newly reimagined space. This is the final gut check.

Once we complete and fill the curio cabinet with the items that hold the greatest value for the client, we take a step back and ensure that the client's most prized items are easily identifiable and include the important written card noting the history of the items. Once the client is satisfied with the completed project, we ask more questions to understand her perspective and feelings about her reclaimed curio cabinet.

Does this space now match the intention you imagined?
Yes. Important sentimental pieces are now easily found in the curio cabinet. I look at them and remember fondly the person associated with the item. I love looking at it now because the important things are in there. My grandmother's few pieces and the Star Wars cups. Before, the cups were all stacked together and now you can see them and enjoy them. It was worth getting rid of the less valuable items in order to see the most important items. Before, I struggled to declutter my sentimental items partially out of fear of getting rid of something that might be valuable. But now I feel that the items I have chosen to let go of can be valuable to someone else.

Does this space now fit your space's function and your current lifestyle needs?
Yes.

M – MAINTAIN your space. Remember that this space will only stay as organized and aesthetically pleasing as you put effort and intentionality into it. Create a plan and a system to purposefully maintain this new space, recruiting any other people needed that utilize or enjoy this space. Accountability is key.

As we neared the end of the seven-step R.E.C.L.A.I.M. process, we wanted to ensure that our client had awareness and a plan of action to continue to maintain this beautiful space. Although this process took approximately two hours to complete, we hoped that this refreshed curio cabinet would continue to showcase this client's most sentimental and prized items for years to come.

What system will you put in place to keep this space as you see it today?

Never adding anything to it. It's perfect the way it is and I'm not touching it. I don't need any more display items. I have more display items and pretty things that aren't even out. If I need a new display item I can pull out an item I currently have hidden.

What steps will you need to take to assure that this space will continue to function and feel like it does right now?

I'm trying to live by the mantra, "If I bring something new in then something needs to go out."

With the client's reframed mindset and reclaimed space in her curio cabinet, this client has a new perspective on how to display and share her beloved sentimental items. The client that once had a difficult time deciding what to keep and what to purge is now capable of deciphering for herself what holds the most sentimental value to her with confidence.

We also want to evaluate how our client experienced the seven steps of R.E.C.L.A.I.M. We asked her the following questions:

How did you feel during the process?
I didn't feel overwhelmed. I thought it went very well. I just sat and looked at things and just analyzed and thought about it. That was easy. If I were doing it by myself it would have taken me longer, and I might not have parted ways with as many items. Just getting the questions asked and critically looking at each item helped tremendously. It helped me determine what I truly valued. You never criticized my decisions or said, "Why are you keeping this ugly thing?" I appreciated that very much.

Was the R.E.C.L.A.I.M. process what you expected it to be?
It was better than I expected because I didn't have to do any heavy lifting. All I had to do was sit and you brought me the piece and I looked at it and thought about it and sometimes you had to ask me deeper questions to get me to say get rid of it or keep it. It helped me to be able to pick up each item and think about it and recall various memories – *Who gave it to me? Where did I get it? What is its significance?* – I found that helpful.

Do you feel comfortable to continue this process now that you have experienced it today?
Oh, yes. If I could get your help again I would be really happy. But now I'm moving full speed ahead. I'm ready to purge.

What advice do you have for others that are unsure about starting or just beginning this process?
It was very worth the time and the input to have a third party be able to ask me questions. I think it helps to bounce things off other people so you're not in a vacuum. Make sure you have the space to spread items out so you are able to look at all the similar items.

FOLLOW-UP

We met with this client to follow up several months later to see how her decluttering journey was going. When we entered her home, it was apparent that she was continuing to make progress.

Now that you've lived with the system for a few months how does it feel?
I feel great. I can now see with clearer eyes and a lot of the things I held on to I'm ready to let go of. I feel good about letting go of stuff.

Do you have any regrets about letting go of any of your items?
No, because I don't need everything my father and mother ever gave me. I don't need everything to remember them. Other family members might be upset, but it's my stuff. My children don't want the items I was passing on, so I have no regrets.

Have you experienced any loss of memories because you donated a sentimental item?
No, not at all.

How has this process helped you reframe your relationship with your things?
I think I need to go back through the two bins I labeled sentimental and get rid of some of the things I've held onto. For example, I have probably seven or eight newspapers from when Man Walked on the Moon in 1969, and I was reading they can have value but I'm not sure that they're all worth saving. They're not in the greatest shape. I've held onto them because my father and I did that together. But I know my father and I did that together from my memory and I don't know that I need the newspapers to reinforce that memory. I have more purging to do.

Have you started to evaluate any other spaces in your home since your first R.E.C.L.A.I.M. process with us?
Yes, the first thing I did was evaluate my books. I have been looking at things with a more critical eye. I am moving full speed ahead with decluttering my entire home. I am ready to purge.

* * * * *

For Your Personal R.E.C.L.A.I.M. Process

We have structured the book so you are becoming more comfortable in your decision-making skills and not second guessing yourself. We started with decluttering spaces that hold less sentimental value so that you have had practice with the Reframe & R.E.C.L.A.I.M. process. This is the chapter where all of that practice will help you make tough decisions with more confidence. Remember that this is *your* process. Take your time and be honest with yourself. As you begin, follow the seven- step R.E.C.L.A.I.M. process below.

We were able to evaluate one of our client's most difficult clutter spots in her home within a matter of hours. If you are deciding to Reframe & R.E.C.L.A.I.M. on your own, remember that decluttering and evaluating your items does not have to be done in one round. It can be helpful to go through and purge the lesser sentimental items first and come back later when you feel prepared to filter through each item with more discernment. This is especially helpful if you find your space continues to feel cluttered as you begin the R.E.C.L.A.I.M. process and is not achieving your aspirational aesthetic intention.

If you do not feel a sense of peace or continue to feel overwhelmed with your space, do a second pass, or even a third, to determine what items truly carry the most sentimental value for you. If you continue to feel stuck in this process, enlist a trusted family member or friend to support you. Set a specific time with the other party so that you have a confirmed allotment of time for their support. With accountability from others, success is more likely to be achieved.

As you navigate your own journey and determine what truly holds value to you, remember that it is important to take your time. For some, it may take hours or even years. Just continue to work through the steps, and trust the process. Recalling the memories of sentimental items is why this process may take longer than the other chapters we explore in this book.

The first step is to know what items you have in your possession. This allows you to start to take inventory. Keeping items boxed up and stored away is a disservice to you and your memories. Reframing how to value, admire, and share these sentimental items and memories of people, places, and things you want to remember will allow you to R.E.C.L.A.I.M. and bring life to the items as well as bring peace of mind for you.

Below are other strategies you can implement when you are considering your personal sentimental items and how to honor these objects and your physical space.

- Old notebooks, letters, and diaries do not take up a lot of space, however photographing, scanning, or creating a digital snapshot of these items can help to preserve the contents from aging and fading.

- Take photographs of the item and give it away. You can still reference the photo of the item to remember, but it will not be taking up the physical space in your home. This can be especially helpful with items that take up large amounts of space.
- Include a small written card with each item in the photograph that encapsulates important information to keep record if desired. Here are possible prompts to document your item.
    - How old were you when you received the item?
    - What year did you receive the item?
    - Was the item a gift or did you purchase it yourself?
    - Who gave the item to you?
    - Where is the item from?
    - Why is the item so special to you?
    - What is the familial significance of the item?
- Would another family member appreciate or enjoy the item and have the desire and space to use it or display it?
- If an organization or individual can use the item, would it be a better manner in which to honor the item?
- For the sentimental items that bring pain and heartache, those bring their own set of mental and emotional challenges to address. We will discuss these items in Chapter 10 in more detail.

If "It's sentimental" strikes a chord with you and you are ready to take action in your space, reference the Tips for Your Personal Reframe & R.E.C.L.A.I.M. Process at the end of our book.

CHAPTER 8

IT BRINGS ME JOY

"My job doesn't spark joy. Can I discard it?"
– Anonymous

Jennifer

Now this excuse is a very slippery slope. I can go through all the other excuses and find reasons to let go of something, but I can justify keeping almost *anything* because it brings me joy. So, how does one decide what brings them true joy? For me, I keep going back to my tried and true questions, *"Would I grab this if my house was burning down?"* or *"Would I pay to have this item moved to my next home?"* and, *"If this item were to be lost or broken would I replace it?"* Asking these questions helps me to define what items bring me the most joy and satisfaction in my home. This clarity allows me to confidently let go of items that I previously justified holding onto because the items brought me some feeling of joy.

As you may have discovered throughout this book, I have always enjoyed traveling. When I travel, I always buy a piece of art or other item that reminds me of my trip. These collected travel mementos bring me joy and remind me of the experiences, fond memories, and adventures I have had in life. Since childhood, I loved seeing the wall maps at each destination I visited. These maps collected pins to represent where other travelers were from. I have always wanted to recreate this same idea in my home to showcase where I have traveled.

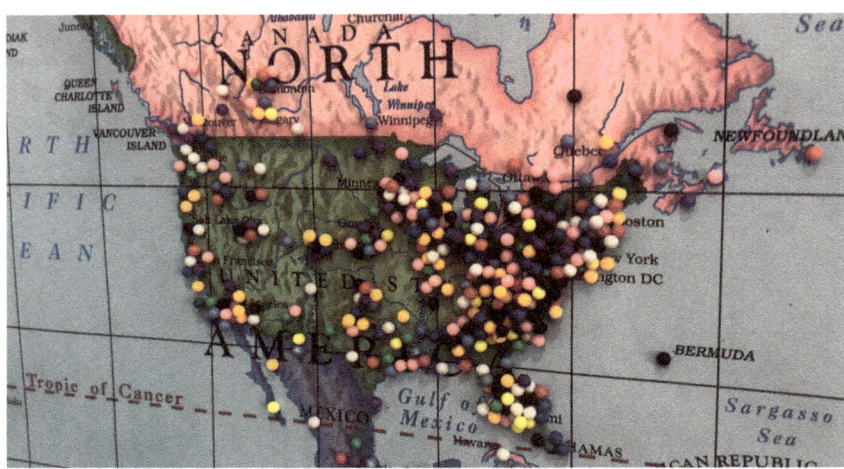

My plan is to eventually visit all fifty states in the United States and all seven continents of the world. I hope to have a map to chronicle all of these travels. That's the hope, at least. I currently have three versions of a United States map sitting on a shelf in my house with the grand intent to make this visual testimony of travels a reality. One map is a wooden map. The purpose is to cut photos into the shapes of the state that I visit and paste it onto the map. This photo collage creates personal memories and a unique and customized map for me to remember my travels visually. Another map is a cork board that mimics the pushpin maps I have seen during my travels. My hope is to layer this cork board map with photos and string, retelling my travel routes. The last map is a much smaller and less personalized United States map made with stickers. Each time I visit a new state I simply peel off a sticker to reveal the state visited.

Now, how long have I had these three maps? Twelve years... TWELVE YEARS! I am forty-three years old. Twelve years is more than a quarter of my life. For twelve years, I have held onto these maps, and these plans that I may or may never use.

Not only are these maps items I may never use, they also remind me of another to-do on my ever growing to-do list. If I travel somewhere new, am I going to add that destination to my map as soon as I get home? *No.* As soon as I return from a trip, I have to unpack, get my kids back on schedule, get myself back on schedule, catch up on emails, restock the groceries, do loads of laundry, and the list goes on. I am going to do all of the essentials, and my map is going to take the lowest spot on the priority list once again. Another obstacle to my personalized travel map project is getting out all my crafting supplies to add one picture to the wooden or cork map, although it would look magnificent and bring me joy and satisfaction. However, the reality is that I will collect a pile of travel photos to get to later.

I justify delaying this project that will bring me joy to a later time when I have more photos and can complete multiple destinations on the maps at once, utilizing my limited time more efficiently. The maps that I hope to bring me joy ultimately create more clutter and more procrastination, equating to more personal stress. The idealization that these maps will bring me joy is overshadowed by the time and space needed to create these personalized travel maps.

It is only when I raise the priority of a project that it turns into a reality. Because of this, I've had to come to terms with what I valued more and what brought me the most peace and joy. There are a limited number of hours in the day and an unlimited number of items on my wish list of life. For some people, the creative process and joy they receive is worth the time and effort to complete a project like this. For me, I realize it is more important to get back to my family's daily routine quickly. I can receive the same amount of joy by saving my photos digitally and having easy access to these memories. Seeing a hanging unfinished wall map was bringing me more stress and frustration than I realized.

The solution to my problem was to instead purchase a world map that I can easily scratch off the places I have traveled to in less than five minutes. I feel satisfied allocating and prioritizing this short amount of time when I return home from a new destination. This satisfies my hope and joy in creating a visual catalog of travel destinations while adhering to my realistic time limitations.

I also love decorating for the holidays and can easily go overboard. It brings me joy to change my home environment to match the spirit of the season and create a feeling of festivity. We have clearly established I have a problem with this as recalled with my seasonal pillow collection from Chapter 2.

In my previous career, I was a product designer for several large retailers, and I designed mainly seasonal products and home decor. When an item I designed was available for sale, I proudly purchased one, if not several. Needless to say, my home quickly filled with items I designed and brought me joy. However, I was unable to keep each and every item I created and purchased in my home. These joyful creations quickly grew to overwhelming storage and clutter issues in my home. Nevertheless, my joy for holiday decorating has yet to diminish.

Realizing that my family functions best with structure and consistency in our everyday life, I have limited my holiday interior decor. For example, I decorate the space above my kitchen cabinets so the home still has the festive feel that brings me joy, but the kitchen counters remain clear for everyday functionality. I have also invested in banners and hanging wall pieces that add color and cheer to the atmosphere while keeping decorations off of the flat surfaces.

Previously, I have decorated two interior Christmas trees, one for my more sophisticated adult aesthetic and one for the mix-matched ornaments collected throughout the years, including my kids' homemade ornaments. I quickly learned that expensive, breakable ornaments do not mix well with curious toddlers. As my kids have grown, I also discovered that they enjoy having space to run and play inside without a large Christmas tree blocking their path. I also feel less anxious with the tree removed because I can let my boys run and be kids instead of worrying about ornaments being knocked off or broken. The kids have a safe space to play and the Christmas tree has been relocated to a more appropriate space for my family and the function of our home.

Today, I choose to display one eclectic tree inside with all our family ornaments, and I have given away all of my fancier breakable ornaments to accommodate my current life with small children. Another reframe I found for myself and my family was to use my once indoor fancy white Christmas tree outside to create a festive secondary living space. The thought of letting go of my beautiful tree was upsetting at first; however, I love indoor/outdoor living and I used my creative side to think outside of the box and outside of my home. I created a solution that allows me and my family to not only enjoy the holidays inside our home, but having this tree in our outdoor living area has brought our family more joy and time outdoors together. This has created balance and has helped our family to appreciate the holidays while maintaining our daily routines.

Reading is a pastime that once brought me joy, but my bookshelves quickly filled with all the great literature and self-help guides I told myself I would get to one day. The reality is I have moved at least ten boxes of heavy books every time I relocated to a new house. At each home, the books simply sat unread and became dust collectors on bookshelves or in the unpacked boxes in my garage. These unread books were not giving me the knowledge or entertainment I was hoping to acquire from them.

I realize in my current life chapter, I no longer have the luxury of reading a book uninterrupted. The time I do find quiet in my home is right before bed when I am mentally exhausted from the day. By bedtime I have no desire to trade my precious hours of sleep for reading. To find the joy I was missing from my paperback novels, I have reframed how I enjoy reading. I do have time to listen to an audiobook while I am doing dishes or folding laundry. Because of this, I have traded my physical copies of books for digital versions that I can listen to when my time allows throughout the week. This gives me much less clutter in my home and in my mind.

Now my cluttered bookshelves are cleared and can be used to store and display other joyful items. Plus my books are readily available for me in digital form. I still love the feel of holding a book and the satisfaction I get from turning the pages. However, for my current chapter of life, a digital format works best so I can gain knowledge and be entertained, which were my goals in the first place. Listening to audiobooks throughout the day has rekindled my joy in reading again, and I have actually listened to more books in the past eighteen months than I have in the last eighteen years.

In the future, when I'm an empty nester, I may find time to sit and read an entire physical book from cover to cover. I may choose to purchase a new sophisticated tree with breakable ornaments or I may choose to travel for the holidays, visiting my kids and enjoying their home holiday decorations. I do not know what the future holds, but by letting go of the items that I am not using in this chapter of my life, it will make it easier to navigate the next chapter when I get there.

REFRAME

"When you're looking at what to bring into your home, or what to hold on to, there's only one question you should ask: 'Will this item help me to create the life and the home I want?'"
– Peter Walsh

Courtney

Finding joy in life is something we all strive to achieve. Joy uplifts us, motivates us, and allows us to feel optimistic and fulfilled. Who doesn't want to find joy in their life? The challenge comes when we continue to chase joy in stuff, without contentment in ourselves. How much stuff is enough to help us feel happy without overwhelming us and our space?

Chasing joy is a slippery slope in life. We feel joy when dopamine, or our pleasure hormone, is released in our brain. This hormone is released when we do something that our body finds pleasurable or fun; however, this hormone is only temporarily released, causing our bodies and brains to seek out more of the pleasure in life. This dopamine rush is something that some find addictive and continue to seek in life, whether it is eating our favorite foods, finding another activity, or purchasing another item to help us feel good. When we fill our space with items to bring us joy, it brings a rush of dopamine, although this rush will continue to be chased.

While we all share the same chemical reaction in our brains, the means in which we fill ourselves with satisfaction and joy varies by each individual. Some may find joy in collecting items. These items fill a small part of their lives with the satisfaction of possessing something that they deem valuable, pleasurable, or joyful. These items span from collecting a rare or special item such as a collectible coin or artifact from history to the newest released shoe to the latest version of technology. Other items may seem more simplistic, yet still bring joy to the owner. These items can be a child's rock collection or a collection of seasonal decorations. These tangible items attempt to fill a space that feels lacking for the individual and brings satisfaction and joy to possess.

Others may collect memories. These sentimental moments can bring a flood of emotion and joy and may be encapsulated by souvenirs from a place visited or a photo from a moment in time. However, each souvenir purchased and kept can also bring burden to someone attempting to find space to display and store each of these items. Although each of these items may bring joy, they can also overwhelm and overfill our space. So what do we do when we find ourselves in these circumstances?

In psychology, joy is defined on a larger scale, enveloping feelings of happiness, acceptance, and harmony. This definition of joy differs from the sometimes fleeting and temporary moments that create a short-lived dopamine rush in our brain and body. True fulfilling joy is found in accepting yourself and your circumstances, within reason. I have worked with hundreds of clients over my almost twenty-year practice in mental health. Reflecting, exploring, and discovering true joy in life comes from a deeper relationship with yourself. Fostering the deeper and more authentic joy in oneself comes from understanding your inner world and reframing negative thoughts and beliefs. Creating an accepting and compassionate relationship with yourself and others, making sense and meaning of your life, and connecting with yourself and others on a deeper level all are essential in finding authentic joy in life. Reframing our mindset and training our brains to find contentment and joy in ourselves, rather than our belongings, is a helpful but sometimes challenging feat.

The challenging yet helpful place to start is looking at ourselves and our environments. I hope most people can say that the items they have chosen to keep in their possession have brought joy or happiness to them in some way. How do these items bring us joy and what amount of joy does each item in our space bring us? In life, it is impossible to keep everything that has once brought us joy and continue to collect more items that bring us joy. If your space is 300 square feet or 3,000 square feet, space is limited in some capacity. So when do we decide what to discard and how to discard the items that bring happiness or joy to our lives? The ultimate answer is to find true joy within ourselves, with or without our stuff, which is easier said than done.

Stopping to reflect about how you feel about yourself and your life can be a first step in understanding what and why things bring you happiness and joy. This is a process for everyone. However, the first step is to take time to reflect and be introspective. Get to know yourself on a deeper level by asking yourself some of the following questions.

1. What brings you joy in life?
2. What are your deepest values?
3. What makes you feel great about yourself?
4. When do you feel the most like yourself?
5. How do you know when you are being completely authentic? When did you last feel that way?
6. What desires keep tugging at your heart?
7. What is on your bucket list?
8. Walk around your home. What clues does it reveal about what you love?
9. What is missing from your life? From the world?
10. What would you regret not doing, being, or having in your life?

This is a great first step in beginning to understand yourself on a deeper level. Although these questions are insightful, some may find it more helpful to work with a mental health professional. It can be a wonderful growth process to talk with a therapist to unpack and explore topics on a deeper level. Support from a trained professional can facilitate the process and support you in finding authentic joy in yourself and in your life.

REFRAMING QUESTIONS

1. What is my motivation in acquiring these items?
2. Do these items bring me joy or does it feel like a task that needs to be completed?
3. What space am I currently using to store or display my collection of items now? Does the collection bring me joy or stress when I reflect on the physical space it currently occupies?
4. Do I have the real estate in my home/space to acquire more?
5. Do I have adequate financial resources to continue acquiring more?
6. How much time and energy do I invest in growing my collection?
7. Does the amount of time and resources I spend on my collection of items allow me to live a life that is fulfilling?
8. Do my collecting habits cause stress for others in my household?
9. How will I know when my collection is complete? Is there an amount of items that will allow me to feel satisfied to stop collecting more?
10. Once this collection is complete, will I be done collecting or will I start another collection?
11. Can these items be rearranged or displayed differently to create newness and joy without having to buy more items?
12. Do I find more prioritization of my possessions over personal needs or social relationships?

R.E.C.L.A.I.M. Case Study

It Brings Me Joy

The client for this chapter is an avid cosplayer who finds joy in acquiring costumes, accessories, and wigs for her cosplay hobby. She was introduced to cosplay during her college experience when she attended her first cosplay convention in 2013. This convention sparked her interest and grew her hobby for seven years until the COVID-19 pandemic took away the opportunities to attend in-person conventions, limiting her creative outlet and connection to the online cosplay community.

Being isolated from the outside world created loneliness and sadness, but the client found a cosplay community on social media, creating a virtual community for her to continue her hobby. The connection to others that shared her love of cosplay helped her build a community at a time when she felt alone. Her interest and focus in collecting more costumes, accessories, and wigs grew to its peak during this time, building her community and joy.

With quickly changing social media trends, her costume collection constantly evolved as she acquired more character costumes than she was able to actualize in her virtual community. Changing character trends, creating original characters, and accumulating multiple versions of the same character caused her to accumulate hundreds of costumes, accessories and over one hundred wigs to satisfy her ever changing creative visions.

Although she is creative, she admits to not having a sewing skillset. Because of this, she purchased most of her costumes online. If the costume did not fit properly or if only one part fit, she purchased more items rather than exchanging for an appropriately sized or new costume set. She also found herself with multiple versions of costumes for the same character and frequently upgraded to higher quality costumes for her favorite characters. The older costumes and items she never returned amounted to approximately a quarter of her total costume collection, taking up valuable real estate.

As the COVID-19 pandemic lockdown was being lifted, she began to return to her daily work routine. She worked remotely from home, sitting behind a computer. Her energy was drained from the long hours behind the computer screen and felt less motivation to interact with her virtual cosplay community.

Currently, she continues to attend conventions and participates in charity cosplay communities, but she is less involved with the social media cosplay community. Cosplay continues to bring her joy, although she is more selective in choosing her favorite characters and costumes. Her cosplay characters are now focused on quality of character and costume rather than quantity of characters and costumes.

Our objective is to evaluate two large closets, and three rolling racks intermixed with everyday and cosplay clothing. The combined hanging clothing space totals 322" (26', 8") of real estate. Returning to the average cost per square foot in a home of $288 from Chapter 2, this client is spending over $7,600 to store her cosplay costumes and clothes.

Before we started the Reframe and R.E.C.L.A.I.M. process, we asked a few questions to better understand our client and her perspectives.

What have been the obstacles for you in assessing and evaluating the items you want to address today?

I think the biggest obstacle is the fact that a lot of these costumes and accessories were never used. I've been holding on to it for so long and I haven't done it yet. I don't have the time anymore, so I should just let it go. There's also so many different versions and variations of certain characters that I have to pick my favorites. Or I ask myself, *Could I ever wear this to a convention?* I know I probably won't wear all of these things again, but I still keep them.

How long have you been accumulating the items we will be reviewing today?

I accumulated most of them over five or six years, and most of them probably haven't been used in one or two years.

How do you feel when you see this space today?

There are a lot of regular clothes mixed in with the costumes. I feel overwhelmed and ask myself, *Why do I have so many clothes?* The cosplay unintentionally bleeds into your everyday clothing because you can take regular clothes and theme them to a character. So a lot of outfits and accessories have been accumulated because I think I could use this piece in a full costume or I could use it to make a modern-day version of a character.

How do you feel now with us here to start the Reframe & Reclaim process?

Really good. Hopefully I can get rid of some stuff and finally feel like I can have all my stuff organized, and it won't sit here doing nothing.

Is there anything about this process that you think may be uncomfortable for you?
Some of these items might bring back memories that I don't want to think about. I've made friendships through social media, but friendships don't always work out. Looking at some of these might bring back memories of certain friendships and characters. Or they might remind me of cosplays I did with my ex. But overall, I don't think it's going to be bad. It will just bring back memories.

As we start the R.E.C.L.A.I.M. process, we will go through the seven-step process below:

R – REFLECT on the current space.

What is your hope for the functionality of this space?
I hope to have the bedroom not be consumed by costumes, and to be able to use the things I've bought. I hope there's more structure and it is better organized so I can quickly grab a costume I need.

How do you hope to feel when you see this space once the Reframe & Reclaim process is complete?
Relief. Clean. Organized. And everything has its place.

What are your hopes in going through the editing and decluttering process?
I hope to get rid of lots of stuff I know I'm not going to use. I want to narrow it down to what I know I'm going to use the most and what I know I will use for an upcoming event.

What's given you the inspiration to start this today?
I want to condense my collection. I'm not on social media as much, and I'm not using a lot of the items anymore. I don't want my cosplay to take up as much space. I feel wasteful when I'm not using my cosplay collection. It can bring joy to someone else.

E – EVALUATE each item and understand the true value each item has for you as you empty the space. Reimagine how this space functions. *How does each item fit into your aspirational space? Does each item match the feel and function you imagined for the space?*

When evaluating the client's clothing and costumes, we choose to bring the clothes and costumes to her on an extra rolling rack in a different room and then have her sort through the items. We created three categories: Keep, Donate or Sell, and Trash.

As the client starts to evaluate her clothes, she quickly makes decisions about each item. In twenty-eight minutes, the client sorts through two closets of clothes and fills three bins with ninety items to donate or sell. What the client thought would take hours to evaluate took less than thirty minutes.

As we continue to work our way through the racks of costumes, the client enjoys remembering events she attended. She stops to talk about the evolution of the characters and how she has learned to style each one. She is able to easily confirm the items she loves and what clothing she is ready to let go of to allow someone else to enjoy the cosplay experience.

Client: I'm feeling really good, and I am excited that someone else will be able to wear it and enjoy it.

How does it feel to see this stuff leaving your space?
Amazing. I don't have to think about it just sitting there in the closet, not being used. I was surprised about how many everyday clothes I was able to get rid of, too.

How does each item fit into your aspirational space?
They fit in the space better. I previously had items in multiple rooms and it's so nice having everything fit in one space.

Does each item match the feel and function you imagined for the space?
Yes. I think because these items already bring me joy. I don't think it matters that there are fewer items because it's quality over quantity. I've narrowed my costumes down to my favorites and I know I will wear them again.

By the end of evaluating all of the client's cosplay and daily clothing, the client chooses to let go of 141 items. A total of six bins of clothing and costumes are donated. The total Evaluation process only took this client one hour and fifteen minutes to evaluate two closet spaces and three rolling racks filled with clothes and cosplay costumes. As the facilitators of the R.E.C.L.A.I.M. process, we were even surprised at how quickly this evaluation process took for the client.

C – CLEAN the space. Empty and clean the space so that it feels like a fresh, clean slate.

How do you feel seeing this space empty versus how you felt with the space occupied with items?
It doesn't feel real. I'm used to it being full of stuff. It feels spacious and open. We went through the items so quickly. It's a relief.

L – LAYOUT and label the space before placing any items back into the space. Attempt to create a blueprint of how the space will look and feel. Measure and readjust the space to fit the space's new functionality, as well as any organizational materials that you may include to enhance the aesthetic and functionality.

What do you hope this space will be for you now that you have reflected and evaluated the items in this space and the space's function?
An organized space I can find my costumes and just grab and go.

A – ASSEMBLE items back into the space and adjust as needed. Allow for trial and error as you reimagine the space's blueprint. This may be adjusting materials, changing where items are located, or reframing what items are truly intended for this new environment.

This client has a wide assortment of costumes and accessories including hoop skirts, large princess ball gowns, heavy cloaks, wigs, hats, bejeweled crowns, jewelry, archery accessories, and lightsabers. After the evaluation process, the client is able to eliminate the largest hanging rack, creating space for her jewelry armoire and shoe rack in between two of the hanging racks. She can now store her cosplay shoes and jewelry in one cohesive space.

On the two remaining rolling racks, we create sections and organize her costumes into multiple cosplay categories: Superhero, Princess, Miscellaneous, and Outerwear, including coats and cloaks. We use aesthetically pleasing heavy-duty wood hangers for her heavier cosplay costumes to ensure they are hung and viewed appropriately.

We reorganize her everyday closet, which now has plenty of room for all of her clothes. As we assemble the items back into her closet, there is newly freed-up space to create a hanging section for some of her licensed backpacks that portrayed several characters from the costumes she collected. We change out the existing mismatched hangers to thin, matching, no-slip hangers in her closet for a pleasing and visually calming aesthetic. The space is now appropriately divided into cosplay and everyday sections, so she can easily view and access what she needs in her space.

I – INSPECT the space once everything is reassembled. Step back and take inventory, viewing the aesthetic and functionality of the newly reimagined space. This is the final gut check.

Does this space now match the intention you imagined?
Yes. It looks way better. Walking in, it feels more spacious. I'm happy with the items I've decided to keep.

Does this space now fit your space's function and your current lifestyle needs?
Yes. It still feels like me but it is not overwhelming. It feels nice. It's controlled chaos. It's not chaotic in the sense it is messy but it is chaotic because it is a lot. But it is not as much as it was. So it's controlled creativity.

REFRAME & RECLAIM

M – MAINTAIN your space. Remember that this space will only stay as organized and aesthetically pleasing as you put effort and intentionality into it. Create a plan and a system to purposefully maintain this new space, recruiting any other people needed that utilize or enjoy this space. Accountability is key.

As we neared the end of the seven-step R.E.C.L.A.I.M. process with this client, we wanted to ensure that our client had awareness and a plan of action to continue to maintain this beautiful space she had helped to create for her home.

What steps will you need to take to assure that this space will continue to function and feel like it does right now?

Just make sure I'm putting things where they belong and sticking to that. Which is hard for me. Keeping it structured. Going forward I will be more decisive and ask myself, *Do I really need this?*

We also want to evaluate how our client experienced the seven steps of R.E.C.L.A.I.M. We asked her the following questions:

How did you feel during the process?

The process was tiring, but it wasn't as overwhelming as I thought it was going to be. I felt a lot of different things. Relief, a little bittersweet because these are things I really love. So there are memories, but at the end of the day, I'm happy with what I kept.

What advice do you have for others that are unsure about starting or just beginning this process?

Get a good night's sleep beforehand or drink more coffee. But seriously, take the step to do it. Trust your gut on the things you're going back and forth between. Just let it go. Even if you are hesitant, once you take the first step, it becomes a lot easier. Even if you declutter a little at a time, it will be worth it in the end.

FOLLOW-UP

After a few months, we contacted the client to check-in with her perspective of the R.E.C.L.A.I.M. process and to find out if she had made more progress. We are curious about how she feels about the amount of items she chose to sell and donate during our time with her. We also wonder if she has any regrets about the decisions she made.

Now that you've lived with the system for a few months how does it feel?
Feels great. It feels less cluttered and more organized. It gives me motivation to keep the space clean.

Does it still work? Anything you would change?
I don't think so. We organized it well. Maybe in the future I will condense down more, but for now there's nothing I need to change.

Do you have any regrets about letting go of any of your items?
I will admit there were a couple times I have been thinking about, *Oh, this would have worked with that item I gave away*. But at the end of the day it's fine. If I really need it I will go buy it again but right now it's just not a high priority and that's okay.

How has this process helped you to reframe your relationship with your things?
I prioritize better and know what doesn't need my attention. I did have those moments of regret but at the end of the day I know this is better because it's less cluttered, more organized, and I know which characters I cosplay more. I think I got so caught up in the cosplay world it was more quantity over quality and now I focus on quality. I know the characters I'm good at and what I want to do.

Have you started to evaluate any other spaces in your home since your first R.E.C.L.A.I.M. process with us?
I have since gone through and reduced the number of wigs I own. I was able to donate ninety-one wigs to a battered women's shelter. It felt really good to get all of the wigs out of the house and I'm glad they are going to get some use for a good cause.

* * * * *

For Your Personal R.E.C.L.A.I.M. Process

We hope that your home is already filled with items that bring you joy. However, many people find their home overflowing with so much joy that it hinders the everyday functionality of their home. With the example of the pillows in Chapter 2, evaluate what items bring you joy and take into consideration how others relate to your joyful items. This will help you better assess the items that contribute to the aesthetic and functionality of your space. We challenge you to reframe how you think about these items and honestly ask yourself the following questions:

- How can you reframe your relationship with your joy-inspiring items to reclaim more real estate in your home?
- How can you reframe how your items bring you joy and contribute to the functionality of your space?
- Is your joyful item creating more stress in your home?
- Is the item that brings you joy currently stored away in a box? If so, how much joy is it really bringing you?
- What things bring you the most joy and fulfillment in life?
- How can I feel the same level of joy with fewer items?
- How can you focus your items to create an environment where they can be enjoyed on a daily basis?

One of the most helpful strategies for joy-related items is to reframe how you view joy and to consider other ways to enjoy these items in your home. When you reflect on and evaluate the items in your home that bring you joy, you can hold on to the value of the items while saving space and reframing how you use or display each item. Below are strategies to help you still enjoy the items in your home but reduce the physical footprint they take up.

USE TECHNOLOGY TO HELP DISPLAY AND STORE YOUR JOY-FILLED ITEMS

How can I use technology to help preserve the excess items that bring me joy? For those with digital photos on your phone, the cost of a cloud backup service may be less than the amount of anxiety you may feel if you were to possibly displace these images. For those who love their collection of movies or music, you can reframe how to access and store these joy filled items with the possible solutions listed below:

- Use digital photo frames to replace physical photos
- Upload photos to your television or computer screensaver
- Upload music to an online server to reduce the physical space your music occupies (iTunes or YouTube Music)
- Subscribe to a music streaming service (Spotify or Sirius)
- Subscribe to a television or movie streaming network (Hulu, Netflix, Disney Plus, HBO Max, Paramount, etc.)
- Create an online drive to store movies (Plex or Embry)
- Utilize a digital book library (Audible or Kindle)
- Use technology to help preserve and back up favorite photos (iCloud or External Hard Drive)
- Create shared to-do lists, wish lists, and bucket lists to help achieve your goals (Notes, Google Drive)

All of these strategies are great tools to help reduce the physical space items occupy as well as create a more organized and accessible way to utilize these items. The above strategies are a starting point to find the systems that best fit your lifestyle needs.

CREATE A BOOK TO DOCUMENT AND PRESERVE YOUR JOYFUL ITEMS

As you evaluate each item, assess how it brings you joy. *Does the item remind you of a happy memory? Does the item remind you of someone in your life? Is it possible to feel the same amount of joy without physically possessing this item?* You can create a physical book with images or a digital catalog of items for you to access on several online platforms such as Shutterfly or Canva. Additionally, it is much easier to fit a book into a fireproof safe than an entire bin of childhood toys, trophies, or awards.

- Take pictures of your childhood toys and create a book including the photos and memories associated with the items. You can capture the memory of these items as well as continue the joyful power of donating these toys to children that can bring life back to these toys.
- If you are an athlete and have accumulated medals, trophies, and certificates you want to keep, take photos of the awards to keep a history of your accomplishments.
- Keep a record of kids craft projects and artwork with photos and create artwork photobooks for you and your children to remember.
- Preserve family recipes by taking photos or scanning recipe cards into one collection. Not only will this preserve each precious recipe, you will also be able to share the important recipes easily with others.

LET YOUR JOY-FILLED ITEMS SERVE DOUBLE DUTY

- Instead of having your favorite books or collection of movies hidden on a bookshelf can you stack them horizontally and use them as a display riser.
- Purchase a frame that not only displays your kids artwork but also stores artwork behind the displayed paper that can be easily rotated and updated.
- Use a rock from your rock collection as a paper weight so that you can enjoy it every day at your desk.
- Hang mugs at your coffee station on the wall in the shape of a tree to double as holiday decor.
- Use spare Legos to construct functional desktop items including bookends, pencil holders, or a letter holder.

SHARE THE JOY

Sometimes there is more joy in giving than there is in keeping an item. Think critically and decide which items bring you the most joy that you will use or display on a regular basis. Reflect and evaluate the quality of the items and if they will stand the test of time between uses. If creating or using your talents brings you joy, finding ways to continue to use your skill sets and share your products or services can bring joy to you and others.

- Regift a book or magazine you enjoyed.
- If you love decorating for the holiday season but have outgrown your festive decor, choose to donate these gently used items to organizations that help to sponsor those less fortunate or in need.
- If you love a pair of shoes but only occasionally wear them, could these shoes be given to someone who will

wear them more often and enjoy their use? Does it give you joy to keep a pair of shoes you love but only occasionally wear?
- If you love gardening but plants are taking over, you can gift someone homegrown flowers or herbs as a gift.
- If cooking or baking brings you joy, choose to make a new recipe for someone in your family or neighborhood and share the meals or sweets with others.
- If you have a skill or trade that you love and brings you joy, offer to teach others a new skill such as crochet, cooking, or woodworking.
- If you have a special talent and want to share your abilities and skill sets with others, you can donate your time or products to organizations to pay it forward.

The goal is to reframe how you fill your home with joy and intentionality. Doing this can transform your mindset and your space. When you evaluate and identify the items that bring you the most joy, it can fill you and your home with more positive energy. By removing the extra items that distract from the items that bring you the most joy, you can highlight your most joyous items.

Start with one drawer, closet, or shelf in your home. It may surprise you how much lighter and happier you can feel in your environment by curating your possessions to fit the function of your personal needs. *What items in your home bring elicit joy and uplift you when you encounter them? How can these items be highlighted and displayed for your space to be filled with positive energy and balance?*

If "It brings me joy" strikes a chord with you and you are ready to take action in your space, reference the Tips for Your Personal Reframe & R.E.C.L.A.I.M. Process at the end of our book.

CHAPTER 9

I'M A COLLECTOR. IT'S FOR MY COLLECTION

"I could stop collecting things, but I'm no quitter."
– Anonymous

Jennifer

If I took a DNA test, I am sure "collector" would be found deep in my chemical makeup. Thankfully, so is organizing. Growing up I collected everything from stickers, rocks, small ceramic figures, and stuffed animals. If there was a set, I wanted to collect every part until my collection was complete. Still to this day, if my kids want a certain toy, I have the urge to find all of the pieces and accessories. Is it the need to ensure that no item is missing? Or perhaps I have inherited the mindset that my job is not finished until I have the entire collection in my possession. Whatever the reason, it is a trait that has been passed down in my family.

Needless to say, I have grown up with the collector mentality and have continued the tradition passed down at least three generations. My mother is retired and spends her summers in Maine and her winters in Texas. She has wanted to remodel her smaller summer home in Maine for years so I suggested for her to move in with my family while she attempts to remodel so that she can sell her Texas home. If she did this, she could potentially downsize her home in Texas and spend more time and attention on her home in Maine. In true collector fashion, she responded that she cannot do this. She has too many "treasures" to downsize and sell her Texas home. Part of me understands this mentality. Another part of me wants to understand what keeps us so connected to our collection of stuff.

Growing up in the 1980s, the Panini Barbie Sticker Album was all the rage. The sticker albums consisted of one book and individually sold packs of six stickers in opaque packaging, creating a mystery of which stickers are waiting inside to be discovered. Children, including myself, were addicted to the thrill of finding a new and unique sticker for their collections. Inevitably, each package of stickers contained duplicates that I already possessed, driving my desire to purchase another package to complete my coveted collection. This strategic marketing ploy and product placement guaranteed me begging for one more pack of collectible stickers at the grocery store checkout line.

At the age of six, this desperation to complete my collection led me to shoplift two packets of stickers from my neighborhood grocery store without anyone knowing. It did not take long for my mother to find my newly stolen sticker packages in my bedroom. My mother required me to return to the grocery store, confess I took the stickers, apologize to the store manager, and pay for the sticker packs I had stolen. I was clearly obsessed because I knew stealing was wrong but I was committed to completing my collection at any cost. After this incident, I learned my lesson and never stole again. Sadly, my sticker collection was never completed. Each time I opened my sticker album, I felt a tinge of disappointment seeing the empty squares where stickers belonged paired with the reminder and feelings of guilt because of my actions.

My love for stickers continued. I had multiple sticker book collections that included Care Bears, Rainbow Bright, Snoopy, Knight Rider, Scratch-and-Sniff, Scratch-off joke stickers, Halley's Comet, and the excess duplicate Panini Barbie stickers. The only purpose of these collections was for me to enjoy looking at them. I have always loved, and continue to love stickers.

As an adult, I collect journaling and planner stickers to decorate my monthly calendar. However, I have modified my sticker obsession since having children. While I used to sit down and devote time to beautifying my weekly calendar, my current chapter of life is spent collecting moments with my kids rather than collecting stickers.

After my grandfathers passed away, I became very sentimental and began collecting handwritten cards and letters that were given to me. I do not keep every card I have ever received, but I focus on cards with a personalized message. I love looking through and comparing different signatures and handwriting styles. There is something so personal yet simple about everyone's signature writing style. After my Dad died, I read through the old cards he had written to me and noticed that he wrote the number 8 as two circles instead of a continuous infinity loop. Because of this, I started writing my eights in this same fashion as a way to remember him. It was a small gesture, but it felt like a secret that continued to connect us after his death. To this day, I continue to hold onto cards that are given to me by loved ones.

Since becoming a mom, I have found new habits and strategies to help myself and my children filter through and simplify our collection of things. I want them to be a part of the process so they don't have the burden of moving and storing items that are no longer useful throughout their journeys in life. I am very proud and shocked that my boys have easily let go of most things we evaluate together. They do not feel the sometimes crippling emotional ties I have felt to items.

For instance, having small children means you will inevitably end up with a never-ending supply of random small toys and found objects to add to their personal collections. However, I do not want them to continue the bad habits I have adopted over the years. The solution for our home, as many brilliant moms have done before us, is to use a small or medium-sized bin to create a physical boundary in which to keep their small toy collections. When the random items begin to overfill the bin, it is time to reevaluate the items and allow each child to decide which items are most valuable to keep. In our home, we use shoe box-sized treasure boxes that my children can now independently go through and evaluate what is most important to them and easily donate items that they choose. This has been a very useful strategy and has expanded my children's decision making skills, allowing them to choose what toys to keep and what toys to give away.

I am attempting to break the cycles of over-collecting and over-consuming for my children. This was not a skill I learned for myself until adulthood. Previously, when a sealed box was sitting in my garage, I created the excuse to not sort through and evaluate the contents of the box because I did not have the time; therefore, the boxes continued to be stored and forgotten. I also did not feel comfortable letting go of the boxes because I did not know what was inside each box. This created a vicious cycle of storing and moving boxes of the unknown.

When I was pregnant with my first child, nesting habits were strong. I had the motivation and made it a priority to finally evaluate my collection of unknown boxes stored in my garage. I decided I cannot keep the items indefinitely if I am only storing them. By taking the time to evaluate each item, I now know exactly what each box contains and reflect if I truly need it or if I am emotionally ready to let it go. If I am not ready, I create an adjustable timeline from three months to one year to revisit and reevaluate these items. Personally, I have found that revisiting items I am not ready to let go of on an annual basis eases the anxiety and fears and allows me to confidently make decisions about my possessions. At the end of the timeline, I re-evaluate each item and have a better understanding of its purpose for my current chapter of life. This is a comfortable yet intentional strategy to evaluate items in several rounds, if needed, and hold me accountable to my long term goals. This is something that twenty-year-old Jen did not know how to do.

REFRAME

*"The line between collection and clutter is razor thin.
Only keep those things that you can display
with honor and respect, the things that bring you joy."*
– Peter Walsh

Courtney

According to *Psychology Today*, approximately forty percent of Americans collect something in life. Not surprisingly, many collectors begin their collecting journey by age ten, shedding insight and awareness that childhood experiences can largely influence the interests and values instilled in young and impressionable minds. As social creatures, we typically learn from others how we belong and how we value our own belongings. Families have a large influence on young minds, and habits easily get passed from generation to generation. For some, the habits that our parents held are learned habits that we continue into our adulthood. "The apple doesn't fall far from the tree," is a cliché for a reason. Genetics and habits can deeply influence our own personal lifestyle habits. For others, if a parent's habits or home environment was distressing or brought discomfort during childhood, they may adjust to distance their own personal habits in adulthood. Some children find dramatically different ways to live than their caregivers in their adulthood.

However, not all family traits are inherited as some find fascination and sentiment in their collecting habits. Collecting can bring feelings of accomplishment and satisfaction when a unique part of a collection is obtained or a collection acquisition is completed.

Whether you are an avid comic book collector, a collector of fine art, or enjoy the thrill of finding hard-to-find and unique stamps from around the world, many people find satisfaction in the hunt and acquisition of their collections. However, collections can grow so large that they can invade the real estate in your physical space as well as your mind.

The collecting process can become an obsession for some – with some people spending overwhelming amounts of time, energy, and resources acquiring the next piece to add to their growing collection. When limited resources are used for the thrill of the hunt, life balance can become unhealthy with some choosing to spend time and money on their collection rather than their own personal well-being. The adrenaline of searching for and finding the newest piece of their collection can be addicting and all consuming. When this happens, the collecting process becomes unhealthy.

The lines can become blurry between healthy hobby collecting and unhealthy hoarding habits. When collecting shifts from intentional collections to obsessive and compulsive habits, challenges begin to arise for the collector. Money resources, time resources, and physical real estate are over-used to collect and store the collections desired. Unfortunately, personal challenges are just the first symptoms of a collector that does not know their limits. Living within their resources and means is challenging. Finding themselves in financial debt due to the drive to collect more, spend more, and find more space to store more creates many obstacles.

Social relationships and work can be affected. Those who over-collect and over-fill their physical space can isolate themselves from others due to feeling overwhelmed or embarrassed. Self-esteem and home hygiene can also become at risk. Keeping up with stuff and keeping their home environment tidy and clean becomes stressful and overwhelming. Organization of collected items can be impossible if their collections are less intentional and curated.

- Have you ever felt an overwhelming urge or compulsion to find another piece to your collection?
- Has that compulsion created challenges in your personal or work life balance?
- Have you lost sleep or forgotten to eat or shower because of your focus on your collection?
- Have you found yourself in financial debt in an attempt to acquire items for your collection?
- Have your friends or family members commented on how large or overwhelming your collection has grown?
- Have you lost friendships or found family relationships more distant due to your collecting habits?
- Has your physical real estate become a storage space for your collection rather than a functional living space?
- Have you felt overwhelmed or embarrassed to have company over due to your collection?

If you are a collector, it can be helpful to ask yourself these questions to better understand the balance and health of your collecting habits. Collections can be a joyful and rewarding pastime; however, many may find themselves in unbalanced and unhealthy relationships with their collections. If you think that you or someone you know may have an addiction to collecting, please find support and resources. There are many support groups and professionals that specialize with helping those with an unhealthy balance in life. Learning to reframe your relationship with your stuff to reclaim the balance of your mind and your real estate can also be rewarding.

REFRAMING QUESTIONS

1. What is my motivation in acquiring these items?
2. Do these items bring me joy or does it feel like a task that needs to be completed?
3. What space am I currently using to store or display my collection of items now? Does the collection bring me joy or stress when I reflect on the physical space it currently occupies?
4. Do I have the real estate in my home/space to acquire more?
5. Do I have adequate financial resources to continue acquiring more?
6. How much time and energy do I invest in growing my collection?
7. Does the amount of time and resources I spend on my collection of items allow me to live a life that is fulfilling?
8. Do my collecting habits cause stress for others in my household?
9. How will I know when my collection is complete? Is there an amount of items that will allow me to feel satisfied to stop collecting more?
10. Once this collection is complete, will I be done collecting or will I start another collection?
11. Can these items be rearranged or displayed differently to create newness and joy without having to buy more items?
12. Do I find more prioritization of my possessions over personal needs or social relationships?

* * * * *

R.E.C.L.A.I.M. Case Study

I'm A Collector. It's For My Collection

Our client is a self-proclaimed collector who has collected various items since she was a kid. She was born overseas and grew up frequently receiving toys to add to her collection from her grandmother who lived in the United States. She collected Barbies, Ninja Turtle figurines, and hundreds of Beanie babies as a child. She remembers her collections as being a fun part of her childhood, but when she relocated to the United States, she was unable to take the majority of her chilchood collections with her.

The client shares that collecting was a pastime in her family. Her mother possessed an extensive record collection and her grandmother had an attic full of collectible treasures that she passed down to family members when she died. Although this client has found satisfaction and joy in collecting throughout the years, as her life and tastes have changed, so have her collections.

Currently, this client and her husband live in a two-bedroom condo with a one-car garage. Due to her limited space, she has created habits of evaluating her collection of items to determine what is truly meaningful and holds the most value to keep in her compact space. Because of this, she has created more miniature collections than large collections of items. For instance, she collects vintage telephones, cameras, and tabletop fans to use as decorations throughout her home. Each of these miniature collections act both as a display and decoration as well as a small curated collection that brings the client satisfaction and joy. Due to the limited space in her home environment, she has created her own rules about the amount of space her collection of items can occupy and does not plan to expand her miniature collections because of the space limitations she creates.

In addition to the miniature collections located throughout her home, she also has a collection of first edition Nancy Drew books that are stacked on a shelf in her living room, and various Starbucks collector mugs. She does not like clutter and does not let her collections get in the way of her everyday living. However, she tells us she will make extra space for her Starbucks mug collection and Nancy Drew books as she acquires more.

For her first edition Nancy Drew books, she plans to purchase more to complete the fifty-six-book collection and has struggled to find a way to display her books. Her collections revolve around nostalgia, and the Nancy Drew books remind her of her childhood joy of reading. She currently has sixteen displayed and has recently acquired an additional thirteen books that are still in the bag from the store.

Her Starbucks mug collection is the largest collection. She first started her mug collection when she worked at Starbucks as a barista. Her collection started with ordinary Starbucks mugs; however, as she found time to travel, she began collecting Starbucks mugs from other cities and countries. She has since gifted and donated the majority of the ordinary mugs to others. However, she continues to grow and collect Starbucks mugs during her travels as mementos and from friends who travel. For this client, these mugs are purely decorative and not used so that they remain in mint condition. She currently has a collection of twenty-two Starbucks mugs from around the world on display above her kitchen cabinets and an additional twenty-five mugs stored in a bin in her garage.

Before we started the Reframe and R.E.C.L.A.I.M. process, we asked a few questions to better understand our client and her perspectives.

What have been the obstacles for you in assessing and evaluating the items you want to address today?
I just haven't had the mental energy to unwrap the mugs in the storage bin since I moved here four years ago. I'm eager to see what's in the bin and rotate out some of the mugs that I display.

How long have you been accumulating the items we will be reviewing today?
Almost twenty years. I started with the local city mugs but as I traveled internationally, my collection grew.

How do you feel when you see this space today?
I still love it. It reminds me of positive memories of places I've been or people that brought the mugs back to me. I forgot I stored so many mugs. I'm excited to see the mugs I've forgotten about.
As we start the R.E.C.L.A.I.M. process, we will go through the seven-step process below:

R – REFLECT on the current space.

How do you hope to feel when you see this space once the Reframe & Reclaim process is complete?
I hope to feel nostalgia seeing my memories displayed in a new way. But I don't think the number of mugs being displayed will change much because of the limited space.

What are your hopes in going through the editing and decluttering process?
To be able to rotate out my mugs. I'd like to include mugs from places I've traveled to with my husband so there is a piece of him up there. I just want to use the space purposefully.

What has given you the inspiration to start this today?
Getting new mugs up there because it has been the same display for the past four years.

E – EVALUATE each item and understand the true value each item has for you as you empty the space. Reimagine how this space functions. *How does each item fit into your aspirational space? Does each item match the feel and function you imagined for the space?*

We begin with evaluating the mugs that are stored in her garage in a storage bin. As we pull them out, we organize them into three categories: to be displayed, potentially displayed, and to store in the bin for her "private collection."

Client: My husband and I just went to Spain and Italy, so those are two mugs I definitely want to display. I want to include the new memories with him.

As we continued to go through the stored mugs she came across a mug from Houston.

Client: I feel like I need this displayed because I'm from Houston. This was probably the first mug I purchased. Yep, it's from 2004. This needs to be out.

In total, it took six-and-a-half minutes to go through her stored Starbucks mugs of which she chose five to be displayed, seven that will potentially be displayed, twelve remained in the private collection storage bin, and one mug was donated. Once we combine the previously displayed mugs with the mugs pulled from the storage bin, we evaluate what she has chosen to display. We decide to wait on choosing additional mugs until we evaluate and assemble how the mugs will be displayed differently.

C – CLEAN the space. Empty and clean the space so that it feels like a fresh, clean slate.

We wash all of the mugs to ensure they remain in mint condition when stored away and look their best when they are on display. We also clean the flat surfaces on top of the cabinets to create a clean surface to refresh the display area.

How do you feel seeing this space empty versus how you felt with the space occupied with items?
I like it empty, but I definitely want the mugs back in their space. I'm excited about the potential new display.

L – LAYOUT and label the space before placing any items back into the space. Attempt to create a blueprint of how the space will look and feel. Measure and readjust the space to fit the space's new functionality, as well as any organizational materials that you may include to enhance the aesthetic and functionality.

The client was displaying twenty-two mugs aligned and equally spaced across two sections of cabinetry. Considering the client's love of mini collections, we purchased clear acrylic risers to create multiple mini-vignettes of mugs. Before assembling the mugs onto the upper cabinets, we played with the layout on the kitchen counter to create four mini-collections. The mini-collections created were: mugs collected during travel with her husband, the original style of Starbucks mugs from the mid-2000s, large print Starbucks mugs, and bright and colorful mugs.

What do you hope this space will be for you now that you have reflected and evaluated the items in this space and the space's function?
I like that it is going to include some mugs from my travels with my husband. I feel like all these mugs are my memories so It will feel better to see places we've traveled to together. I like the idea of staggering the mugs on risers instead of having them in a straight line all the way across. I think it will look less cluttered.

A – ASSEMBLE items back into the space and adjust as needed. Allow for trial and error as you reimagine the space's blueprint. This may be adjusting materials, changing where items are located or reframing what items are truly intended for this new environment.

Once the client decides on the four main mini-collections, we begin placing the risers and mugs on top of the cabinet. Using the risers adds height variations to the mug display to improve the visual aesthetics. The eye is able to move along the objects and can see the city names more clearly. After further assembling, we discover the client is able to fit one additional mug above the oven and kitchen cabinets, eliminating the display space above the refrigerator. The 36" cabinet above the fridge is now clean and empty, allowing the client to regain more empty space that she enjoys in her home. Keeping the mugs on one cabinet with risers also creates a more intentional focal point to view the mugs.

Additionally, the clear acrylic risers can easily be rearranged when refreshing and updating future displays.

In the center of the mug display, we place the first mug she ever purchased, the Houston mug. The original Starbucks mugs she collected from the early 2000s and the set of four mugs that represented their travels together were placed on either side of the Houston mug, centering and bringing attention to her most beloved mugs in her collection.

Client: It's already looking better. Less clutter. Ooh, I like it. I should change it up more often. I didn't even think about displaying it differently. I'm glad you suggested the risers. I never would have thought about it. I added a mug and saved space. It looks so good. I love it. Before the mugs were all in a row and would maybe blend in together. You couldn't even see some of the mugs. Now you can easily see them.

By reframing how she displays her prized collection, she is now able to clearly see and recollect her memories associated with the mugs and her travels. The client is also able to reevaluate which collector mugs she displays in her current chapter of life, to include her husband, and find more space to clear above her refrigerator. The process was simple but impactful for the client.

REFRAME & RECLAIM

I – INSPECT the space once everything is reassembled. Step back and take inventory, viewing the aesthetic and functionality of the newly reimagined space. This is the final gut check.

We move the mugs to the front of the display shelf so that the mugs are easily seen. To ensure the mugs are secure, we take the time to aggressively close the cabinet doors to ensure the collection of mugs stay in place and are not damaged from the daily cabinet use. We then take the time to double check and rotate each mug for the best individual mug position as well as the aesthetic of the entire Starbucks mug collection.

Does this space now match the intention you imagined?
I didn't know what I imagined but yes. I didn't get rid of the mugs I love. I put out some newer mugs, and I think I will be able to very easily rotate out and change the mugs I want to display. It still represents mugs people have given me, places I have traveled to myself, and then places I've been to with my husband.

Does this space now fit your space's function and your current lifestyle needs?
This looks a lot brighter and cleaner. I like it. It's easier to see the mugs and my husband will like that he is now included in the display. I love it. I like the new way to organize it. It's so cute and so simple. I would never have thought of using the risers.

M – MAINTAIN your space. Remember that this space will only stay as organized and aesthetically pleasing as you put effort and intentionality into it. Create a plan and a system to purposefully maintain this new space, recruiting any other people needed that utilize or enjoy this space. Accountability is key.

The entire R.E.C.L.A.I.M. process took four hours and twenty minutes, including a shopping trip to the Container Store. Because this client was thoughtful and intentional about her mug collection, the focus was less about how to reclaim physical space and more about reframing how to display her collection. She created and stood true to the limits and boundaries of her collection so that her collection did not overwhelm the space she lives in.

As we neared the end of the seven-step R.E.C.L.A.I.M. process with this client, we wanted to ensure that our client had awareness and a plan of action to continue to maintain this beautiful space she had helped to create for her home.

What system will you put in place to keep this space as you see it today?
I like the idea of once a year going through all the mugs and rotating and cleaning them. Then I can incorporate any new mugs.

We also want to evaluate how our client experienced the seven steps of R.E.C.L.A.I.M. We asked her the following questions:

Do you feel comfortable to continue this process now that you have experienced it today?
Yeah. I like the reimagining of my collection because I've always displayed them the same way for thirteen years. They have always been displayed in one line across.

What advice do you have for others that are unsure about starting or just beginning this process?
I feel like in general, going through spaces yearly or even taking a small space and going through it every couple months.

Is there anything about the process you would change?
No. I like that it didn't feel like I had to get rid of stuff. It was just, *How can I use this more?*

According to the client, she was pleased with the new manner in which her mug collection was displayed – all the better to tell the story of her travels and memories. It was important to this client to ensure that her loved collection also included her husband and their chapters of life together. A little creativity and openness to reframing her mug collection has created more open space above her refrigerator and a cohesive storyline for her display.

Because this project took less time than we allotted, we utilized this additional time to R.E.C.L.A.I.M. display space for her Nancy Drew books that she has been collecting for eight years. Her last purchase of thirteen Nancy Drew books are sitting in a paper bag on the floor because she does not know where to display them.

Client: Growing up we had the new edition books with the bright yellow covers and that's what I normally find in antique stores. But I randomly found a really old Nancy Drew book. Now, I'm trying to find the oldest books I can. Some books are from the 1930s.

Viewing her current living area layout, we offer to relocate and reframe how her mini-collection of books is displayed by moving some of the other items in this space. We are able to display the entire first edition Nancy Drew books together on her living room console table below her television, where the antique yellow hardback books contrast against the black of the television, highlighting the book collection and creating visual interest. Not only does this reframed layout showcase her current book collection, it also allows additional space for her to continue to add to her joyful collection in the future.

REFRAME & RECLAIM

BEFORE

AFTER

FOLLOW-UP

Six weeks later we checked in with this client to see if she was still enjoying her newly displayed collections. We are hopeful that both the client and her husband are enjoying the reframe of how her collections are displayed in their home.

Now that you've lived with the system for a month and a half how does it feel?
The displays of both the mugs and the books feels fresh and less cluttered.

Does it still work? Anything you would change?
Yes. I haven't changed anything. I like it.

How has this process helped you reframe your relationship with your things?
I think it is good to go through my items and change how things are displayed. It feels fresh and new to rotate the items I have displayed every once in a while.

Have you started to evaluate any other spaces in your home since your first R.E.C.L.A.I.M. process with us?
I have cleaned out my master closet and donated some items. It feels good because sometimes things pile up.

* * * *

For Your Personal R.E.C.L.A.I.M. Process

To help yourself from sliding down the slippery slope of collector's captivity, we must reframe our thought process about collecting.

Identifying your personal values surrounding collecting and creating boundaries for yourself can be a beneficial way to curate your collection and maintain the functionality of your home. As you evaluate your items, keep in mind the following boundaries to keep you on track to achieve your collecting goals.

CREATE A NUMBER BOUNDARY

Give yourself a set amount of items you will allow yourself to add to your collection. Once the predetermined number is met, do not buy more items unless you are willing to let go of an existing item in your collection. This is an example of the one-in-one-out strategy introduced in Chapter 2.

- If you love heels, choose the heels that you will wear most and bring you the most joy. Allow yourself to keep a set number of heels.
- If you collect figurines, create a set amount of items you will display without overburdening your space.
- If CDs or records are your jam, create your own top fifty playlist and only keep those records that make the list.
- Limit the number of pieces you display of your children's art collection and rotate the art pieces.

CREATE A SPACE BOUNDARY

The number of items you can keep may also be determined by the physical space you have available for your collection. Creating a physical size boundary, such as a certain size storage container, can also be extremely helpful in evaluating and curating your collections to your favorite and most functional pieces.

Designate a container, shelf, or cabinet to store or display your collection. If the collection does not fit in the space you have allocated, choose your favorite items to occupy the limited space. If the items you want to keep for your collection do not fit in the designated space, are there other possessions in your home you would part with to make more space available for this collection? When the designated space is filled, take a step back and inspect the amount of space allocated and adjust as needed until you feel content.

- Designate one cabinet to store your dishware collections.
- Limit Spring holiday decor collections(Valentine's Day, St. Patrick's Day, and Easter) to one large bin.
- Allow one area of your home to store your action figure collections that are not displayed regularly, such as a closet or shelf in the garage.
- Store your stamp and coin collections in quality binders with pocket pages or specialized plastic containers designed to keep your collection protected.
- Limit sentimental childhood toy collections to one container to store in your closet or garage.

CREATE A TIME BOUNDARY

If you have trouble deciding if you should keep or let go of an item, give yourself the following time boundary to help decrease your anxiety and increase your confidence in choosing what items to keep. Time can be a helpful tool in giving yourself time to reflect and space to make decisions about your collections.

- If I have not thought about my collection in _____ months/years, I will feel comfortable parting with it.

- I will allow myself _____ months/years to display this collection as it is, and then reevaluate what to keep.
- I will revisit my collection of action figures in _____ years to decide what to display, store, and sell.
- I will allow _____ years to pass then evaluate my collection to decide what to keep and what to part with.
- I will decide in _____ months/years what to do with my collection of baseball cards.

REFRAME HOW YOU DISPLAY YOUR COLLECTION

As you decide which collections and items within your collections are the most important to you, be sure to display them in a way that honors their value. Items and collections that have the highest value need to be displayed and stored in a way that you can enjoy them. Reframing how you store and display your collections can ensure that your collections keep their sentimental and monetary value. Displayed collections that are curated and purposeful can also bring joy to you and others that view your collections.

Use the merchandising techniques that retailers utilize to create visually appealing collections by displaying existing merchandise in new ways. Revisit your displays annually to reimagine and refresh your collection. Reframing and rearranging your collection from time to time can create newness without needing to purchase new items or expand your collection.

- Place your favorite collectibles in a prominent place.
- Rotate the items in your collection to freshen up your display without purchasing more.
- Curate your collection with a placard explaining the origin and importance of each item.

- Play with the heights or cluster items together to add visual interest.
- If your art collection exceeds your available wall space, showcase a curated art piece seasonally. Store the additional art pieces in your private collection.

The items you choose to collect and the space you choose to give to each collection may vary. How you choose to display and store your collections is ultimately up to you. Creating boundaries for yourself can hold you accountable for the size of your collection, space allocated for your collection, and time in which you choose to evaluate and reframe your relationship with your collection.

Collecting is a personal habit that can bring joy and achievement. Staying focused on a healthy balance with your collecting habits and available physical space for your collection can allow you to continue healthy and happy collecting for years to come. However, if your collections are overwhelming your physical space or creating more challenges for you, your home, or your personal resources, it is important to evaluate your lifestyle balance. The slippery slope of collecting can grow to unhealthy hoarding habits that can damage your mental, social, and financial health.

With self-awareness and self-reflection, collectors can continue to find their next treasure with joy and excitement in healthy and balanced ways.

If *"I'm a collector. It's for my collection,"* strikes a chord with you and you are ready to take action in your space, reference the Tips for Your Personal Reframe & R.E.C.L.A.I.M. Process at the end of our book.

CHAPTER 10

THE TRIP THAT DIDN'T GO AS PLANNED

"Does the stuff and things around you represent who you are today, or who you were in the past?"
– The Unclutter Angel

Jennifer

The morning after my father passed away, I had slept in, but I woke up to the sound of my home filled with people. The people that filled my home all meant well. They were there to help my mother cope with the loss of her husband and help her navigate the process of arranging a funeral. My father was relatively young at the age of forty-three and had not yet written a will in the event of his death. Several members of our church were helping clean and tidy our home in preparation for the onslaught of visitors that would soon be coming over to pay their respects. My life had been turned upside down less than twelve hours before, and the last thing I wanted was my house full of people. I wanted to feel like the previous night was just a bad dream and not have to live with the fact that my life would forever be changed. I wanted normalcy. So I did what every kid does the day after a traumatic event. I went to school.

With the unexpected death of my dad, I needed to feel like some part of my life would resume as normal so I kept my regular school schedule and asked my mom to drive me. I decided to take something my father had given me so I could attempt to feel close to him on that day. I chose a small green bear he had won for me at Six Flags when I was six years old. After taking it on a water ride that day, it had gotten wet and soggy. I had hugged it so much while carrying it through the amusement park that the bear had a permanently smooshed face and turned up nose. To anyone else it would look like a tattered bear that was due for an upgrade.

Honestly, before my father's death, I hadn't thought about the bear much in the nine years since he gave it to me, but in this time of crisis this bear was a tangible symbol and connection to my dad. I wanted to cling to a happier time when we were together and attempting to win amusement park games was the most stressful part of the day. Not separated by death.

My mother was hesitant to take me, but when I was adamant that it was what I wanted, she respected my wishes and drove me to school. When we got to the high school office, my mother explained the situation to the administration of my father's unexpected death the previous evening. The administrative secretary also looked at me with hesitation and wanted to confirm it was what I wanted to do. When I confirmed, I was sent to class.

I would get the bear out occasionally to assure myself that it was still in my backpack and give me comfort throughout the day. At the end of the day we had P.E. class. Overall, the entire day was a blur, but I do remember P.E. class. I was sitting up against the wall of the gym with my backpack holding my bear. I had only told my closest friends that my dad had died, but at the end of the day, I did not know how many people had found out.

A girl came up to me and asked if she could see my bear. My gut instinct was to keep the bear in my possession, but she had never given me reason to distrust her. I reluctantly handed it over. She proceeded to chuck it across the gym. After that I remember breaking down and crying. It all came pouring out. I do not believe she knew my father died or that this small green smushed bear was a gift that he had given me. I do not hold a grudge against her, but this event defined the end of a chapter of my life.

My mom was called after this incident. I went home for the remainder of the day and I stayed home for the next two weeks. My life was forever changed. The life path I had imagined had taken a severe turn, and I had no control. All I could do was cling onto what was comforting to me – this little green bear.

Fast forward to 2023, when I was doing a major decluttering session and I had finally decided it was time to go through my childhood toys that my children had no interest in keeping. I was still struggling with being able to completely release the items but by taking a photo of each toy, I would be able to see it and recall the memories associated with it without having it take up the physical real estate in my home. I knew it would be hard so I started with easier items like my Teddy Ruxpin that no longer worked and my Popples bank. Then I moved on to harder items like the rainbow bright doll my grandmother had lovingly handmade for me.

Deep in the bin was the little green bear my Dad had won for me. As I worked through the bin, I could see the bear staring back at me, and my anxiety began to rise as the memories resurfaced from that horrible day. I saved the bear as the last item to evaluate because I knew it would be the hardest item for me emotionally. As I picked up the tattered green smushed bear, a flood gate of emotion was released. I was suddenly reliving all of the emotions I had suppressed from that traumatic chapter of my life. The tears and heartache of twenty-seven years overwhelmed me. This small bear symbolized one of the most significant shifts of my life.

Some might say that this small bear held a lot of meaning, so why not keep it? It was not taking up much physical space. However, the mental weight it held for twenty-seven years was not worth keeping. Part of me feels guilty that this little bear reminded me of so many good memories and also signified one of the toughest days of my life. I chose to let go of this little bear, but hold onto the gratitude that this object was able to help me through my father's death. Although I let go of this object, the good memories the bear signified have not faded, however, I now am free of the physical reminder of that terrible day. There are still plenty of heavy memories I retain, but this one I can let go of and feel relief.

REFRAME

*"When we clear the physical clutter from our lives,
we literally make way for inspiration
and good, orderly direction to enter."*
– Julia Cameron

Courtney

Life can be unpredictable. We hope for the best and attempt to make the decisions in life that best suit our vision and dreams; however, we have very limited control in life. One thing I tell my clients frequently is that we can only control ourselves. Whether it is our words, our behaviors and decisions, our friendships we choose to nurture, or our partners we choose to marry, there is only so much that is in our control. I do not believe anyone that chooses to marry also plans for a divorce; however, present day statistics report that over half of all marriages in the United States will, unfortunately, end in divorce.

Friendships that we connect with in our adolescent years may continue to thrive and grow, however, it does take more than one person to ensure that these relationships last through the chapters of our lives. There are also outside factors and variables that some do not anticipate. A relocation for a new job, the birth of a new child, financial habits and hopes, or the death of a loved one can shake the ground of so many and their understanding of who they are, who they want to be, and who they are becoming.

The hope is that the journey of life takes each individual on what one hopes will be fulfilling and hopeful; however, there are unexpected twists and turns, obstacles and detours, and sometimes a dead end. Heartache, unexpected losses, and trauma can undoubtedly bring a more complex and challenging layer to life. These endings can feel like a loss, devastation, and hopelessness; however, these life changes may also bring newness and possibilities if we allow ourselves to reflect, reframe, redirect, and become resilient. Although this process does take time, allowing yourself to go through the emotions and attempt to make the best understanding of these events, can create a path of positive change and personal growth.

So what do we do when one chapter along our life's journey ends? How do we make sense of our own journey through life when a friendship, career, or marriage has changed, fizzled, or ended? Many people struggle with their identities as they move from one chapter of life to another. Change is challenging. Redefining ourselves in life, reframing and redirecting our life journey can stretch us and also grow us.

These past chapters are not failures, and you are not a lesser person for enduring them. Everyone has chapters of life that they wish to repress or erase. Some life chapters are longer than others. Other chapters are converted to CliffsNotes because we do not want to deal with the heartache and pain. So we put those memories in a box and store them away.

Reframing our mindset surrounding these obstacles can allow us to reframe our identities among unexpected life changes. When we do this, we can learn how to claim a new or evolved identity and claim a new path and direction in life.

REFRAMING QUESTIONS

1. Do I want to keep this item in my possession?
2. Does keeping this item help me in my current life chapter?
3. If this object were not in my possession, would I still remember the memories of this time, person, or place?
4. Is this object something I hold sentimental value in? Or does this object hold more sentimental value to someone else?
5. How can I honor and recall the important moments or people associated with this item if this item were not in my possession?
6. If the sentimental value is due to someone one else valuing this object, why do I feel obligated to keep this item? Is this felt obligation something I would expect of someone else?
7. Can anyone else find value or purpose in this item besides me? If so, could this object be more useful for someone else in their possession?
8. How would I feel knowing the object would be used more often than I am currently using it? Would that make a difference?
9. When do I imagine myself using this item again?
10. If given the opportunity to use this item in the future, would I choose this item or a possible different but similar item?
11. What space am I currently using to store this item now? Can this space be better utilized in another way?
12. What timeline do I give myself to use this item before I decide to let go of it?
13. Is there someone else that can use this item if I am not realistically going to use it in the near future?

* * * * *

R.E.C.L.A.I.M. Case Study

The Trip That Didn't Go As Planned

The client in this chapter has an extra room that has been converted to a storage area for extra items in her home that she no longer needs or has yet to use. The room is the only upstairs space, above her garage, that is separate from her other living areas downstairs. It was once used as a music room but has become a storage room for the extra items in her home. It has also become a storage area for her ex-husband's property that he has not yet claimed from their once-shared home.

How long have you been accumulating the items we will be reviewing today?
Almost twenty years. I was eighteen, and we were just moving it from that place to this place.

How do you feel when you see this space today?
Just overwhelmed with the amount of space that is being consumed by the things I don't want. It could be a cool space that I could actually use but first, I have to get everything out that I don't want or need. And the lighting in the space is not that great.

How do you feel now with us here to start the Reframe & Reclaim process?
I feel motivated. I feel like this is going to help me jumpstart.

Is there anything about this process that you think may be uncomfortable for you?
I don't know. It has been a year and a half since our relationship ended. I think we're going to find out.

As we start the R.E.C.L.A.I.M. process, we will go through the seven-step process below:

R – REFLECT on the current space.

How is this space currently being used?
Storage, basically. I don't really have the need to go up there unless I'm running out of space downstairs. So it just ends up being a catch-all for everything that I don't have room for downstairs. I'm storing everything from frames, to excess furniture that I really don't need anymore. There are also mirrors that I was going to use in renovations for my bathrooms that are not yet hung and things I was going to sell.

What is your hope for the functionality of this space?
I had a few ideas. Eventually, I may start a small resell business and sell some purses, shoes, and goods that I have. Maybe that as a staging area and place where I go take the pictures and keep the inventory. Other than that, I haven't thought of it too much.

How do you hope to feel when you see this space once the Reframe & Reclaim process is complete?
I want it to be mine. There's a lot of his stuff, his band things, and things that I don't want. But I want it to feel more of mine. I want the space to feel useful - not just a big open room to hold things that I never go into. I want it to be more tasteful, less clutter. I want it to feel clean, open, brighter, lighter... just better.

What are your hopes in going through the editing and decluttering process?
I hope to get the unneeded items out that are just taking up space, and to create more functional space for me.

What's given you the inspiration to start this today?
I want to make this space mine and no longer ours. I don't want other people's belongings taking up my space anymore. I want to claim this space for myself.

E – EVALUATE each item and understand the true value each item has for you as you empty the space. Reimagine how this space functions. *How does each item fit into your aspirational space? Does each item match the feel and function you imagined for the space?*

We begin the R.E.C.L.A.I.M. process by clearing out the items that are her ex's and placing these items in the garage. We want to ensure that all of his possessions are respected but not taking up space in the room the client is reclaiming. Once the items that do not belong to the client personally are removed, we are able to see the space differently. The client was surprised at how much real estate was revealed as well as her own collection of items that have been stored in this space.

When we started this Reframe and Reclaim process, you thought this was a space that was used for storing your ex's items from the past, but we actually found several of your items.
I found glass containers, votives, and vases. There was a random container in the closet that I haven't seen in years. There's a storage ottoman I hadn't used it nor thought about. It has literally been up here sitting. I have obviously lost interest in these things.

We noticed as you were evaluating some items instead of saying, "Oh, let me look through it," you quickly and decisively stated, "Nah, that can go."

Yeah. I started to look through some items, but then I asked myself, *Why did I keep this to begin with?* I have a box full of frames I have decided to keep. I don't need three boxes full. For many of these frames, I just bought it because it was a good deal. Seeing everything in this room is allowing me to narrow down what I really want versus what I kind of liked in the past.

C – CLEAN the space. Empty and clean the space so that it feels like a fresh, clean slate.

How do you feel seeing this space empty versus how you felt with the space occupied with items?

Good. I can breathe easier. It's empty, bright, clean, and smells better. It definitely feels more like mine. I'm starting to think this might be a room I want to use more.

L – LAYOUT and label the space before placing any items back into the space. Attempt to create a blueprint of how the space will look and feel. Measure and readjust the space to fit the space's new functionality, as well as any organizational materials that you may include to enhance the aesthetic and functionality.

Once the room is emptied and clean, the client begins to see it as a room of possibilities. Before, the boxes and clutter were dictating what the space was, which was a 200-square-foot storage room. Now that the clutter is gone, it is open-ended. It can be whatever she wants for her next chapter and new identity.

What do you hope this space will be for you now that you have reflected and evaluated the items in this space and the space's function?

I am not sure yet. Before it felt very dark, dingy, and just heavy, but it's just a light and airy room now. Now that I'm looking at it in the light, there are definitely some pictures and things that I want to hang. I may make it a reading space. I'm not 100% sure, but I'm loving it. I just want to make it more my style and my personality. I like the light coming in a lot. It's a different vibe for sure.

A – ASSEMBLE items back into the space and adjust as needed. Allow for trial and error as you reimagine the space's blueprint. This may be adjusting materials, changing where items are located or reframing what items are truly intended for this new environment.

Now that the space is ready to be filled intentionally. We discuss how the client wants the items to be displayed in this space. For many years, this space was dimly lit and used as a moody music area. After her ex moved out, it then became a dark and cold storage space. Our hope is to bring light and life to this space.

The client decides to shop for items that match her current chapter of life, combining the themes of boho and coastal aesthetics. Bright lighting, earth tones, and some added cushions and pillows are purchased to add a refreshed and inspiring ambiance to her newly reclaimed room.

With two-and-a-half hours of shopping and two hours assembling the room, we have transformed this place from really dark, really cluttered, and really heavy to light and decluttered. You did not want to come upstairs. It was just a place you went to store things. Now it has functional closet storage, and space to sit and relax.

Yes. And all of my stored things that were up here are out of the way. The things I chose to keep have a functional space in the closets. It no longer looks like a storage unit. It is a huge difference from before.

Now that we've updated the decor, how does it feel now?
It is so much better than I thought it would be honestly. It's very bright, more me, my colors. I'm liking it. I think we knocked it out of the park considering it took less time than I imagined it would.

I – INSPECT the space once everything is reassembled. Step back and take inventory, viewing the aesthetic and functionality of the newly reimagined space. This is the final gut check.

Does this space now match the intention you imagined?
Yes, it is now mine, more of my style. It is lighter and brighter as I hoped it to be. The lighting is everything!

Does this space now fit your space's function and your current lifestyle needs?
Yes. I need it to be versatile to meet my needs in the future. Now, I have space to do that. Since the lighting is improved, I can use this space for photos for my possible resell business. The space feels comfy for sure. It's giving me more ideas of what I want to do with it. This is definitely a good starting point. The possibilities feel open and free.

REFRAME & RECLAIM

M – MAINTAIN your space. Remember that this space will only stay as organized and aesthetically pleasing as you put effort and intentionality into it. Create a plan and a system to purposefully maintain this new space, recruiting any other people needed that utilize or enjoy this space. Accountability is key.

As we neared the end of the seven-step R.E.C.L.A.I.M. process with this client, we wanted to ensure that our client had awareness and a plan of action to continue to maintain this beautiful space she had helped to create for her home.

What system will you put in place to keep this space as you see it today?
I know just to not take on a new project because I already have projects I haven't done. A ccuple years ago I was the type to say, *"I'm going to sell this or I'm going to keep this and make a profit on it or I'm going to flip this,"* but you end up with an office full of boxes and a room you never use anymore. Don't buy it, so you don't have to let it go. Let that be someone else's problem.

What steps will you need to take to assure that this space will continue to function and feel like it does right now?
I've realized that when I was younger I just would buy things. It was a good feeling. or, *"Oh I got this deal, and I'm going to use it one day."* Now I hardly ever go shopping because I'm dealing with the aftermath of that mentality. I don't want to be surrounded by things that are overwhelming me just because at that point it was a deal. It's two different feelings. The feeling you felt when you bought it versus the feeling later when you don't know what you are going to do with the item you bought. It's counter-productive.

So I'm hearing in the moment there is that adrenaline and the excitement of finding a good deal, but then you have a room filled with all this stuff. What was the feeling you had seeing all of the stuff in this room?
It was overwhelming. Just heavy. You have all these things, but they are just in a box. You're not using them and now they are getting broken. I'm obviously not using it. Just get rid of it.

We also want to evaluate how our client experienced the seven steps of R.E.C.L.A.I.M. We asked her the following questions:

How did you feel during the process?
I felt productive. It was not bad or hard. I felt relieved I am actually going through things.

Was the R.E.C.L.A.I.M. process what you expected it to be?
No, it is more. I thought we were just getting my ex's stuff out and giving me more space to eventually work through the other items. Instead, it was like bam, bam, bam – here we are. We're doing it. We ended up making a lot more room in the closets and having a lot more storage.

Do you feel comfortable to continue this process now that you have experienced it today?
Yeah. It's given me more motivation. Just knowing that I can actually be in one of those houses that you see that doesn't have crap everywhere. Now I realize I can have space for everything. All of the space is useful. It's not just taken up by boxes.

What space do you hope to evaluate next?
My office, because it's another decent-sized space that I could eventually keep adding and adding to, and I don't want to keep adding clutter to it.

What advice do you have for others that are unsure about starting or just beginning this process?
Take it a day at a time. Like you said, this took three hours of a day. And they might not have the help like I did today, but take it one day at a time. As long as you're doing something toward your goal you're being productive. Just keep being productive. I think you should also expect the unexpected in a good way.

Again, just ask yourself, *Is it worth having? Are you going to get to it?* Having this much open space is so much better than having all the things.

Any feedback you have for us as we have helped you facilitate this process?
No, it was a lot faster than I thought it was going to be. So thank you.

FOLLOW-UP

This client was navigating a significant transition period in her life when we helped to facilitate her R.E.C.L.A.I.M. process. She was not sure how the new space above her garage was going to be used, but she was open to new possibilities. We are excited to reach out to this client and hear how her space has evolved.

Now that you've lived with the system for a few months how does it feel? Does it still work? Anything you would change?
I feel lighter. The space has remained empty, without clutter. The room was a blank slate, and my mom decided to move in with me. She changed the layout of the furniture to accommodate the functionality of the room for her needs.

Do you have any regrets about letting go of any of your items?
None at all.

How has this process helped you to reframe your relationship with your things?
I have not started any new projects or purchased more things for my house. I am still in the process of clearing more space.

* * * * *

For Your Personal R.E.C.L.A.I.M. Process

Reflecting and evaluating the questions in the previous chapters can be beneficial if you are attempting to make decisions about your possessions and what to do with each item. You can reference each chapter below if you are having challenges related to the following excuses when evaluating the items you have in your space.

- 2: YOU CAN NEVER HAVE TOO MANY
- 3: I MAY USE IT ONE DAY
- 4: IT'S SUCH A GOOD DEAL
- 5: IT HAS VALUE
- 6: IT WAS A GIFT
- 7: IT'S SENTIMENTAL
- 8: BUT IT BRINGS ME JOY
- 9: I'M A COLLECTOR. ITS FOR MY COLLECTION

When evaluating the excuses that accompany your items, be mindful that negative feelings associated with your belongings can be compounded when someone feels obligated to keep an object out of guilt or sense of responsibility. It is critical to evaluate the items and your relationship to the items to truly understand the reason you feel the need to keep an item that holds you attached to a negative past chapter. What steps do you need to take to close this chapter with confidence and true peace of mind?

Use the questions below as a guide to reflect and evaluate each object. Determine the item's value in your current chapter of life.

- What are the reasons you keep the item?
- What do you gain in keeping this item?
- How would you feel if you no longer had this item?
- Are you keeping an item to punish someone else?
- Are you keeping an item to punish yourself?
- Are you able to reframe your relationship with an item without past negative feelings associated with it?

If the items that you are holding on to are from a past unexpected life chapter, it can help to journal, talk to a friend or family member, or explore your feelings with others. However, If you are having difficulty identifying a reason you continue to find yourself stuck in the past chapter of life, contacting a professional counselor can be beneficial for you to gain awareness. Being honest with yourself and speaking to an objective professional counselor can be beneficial. Death loss, relationship loss, job loss, traumas, and other chapters that we have little control over can create feelings of self-criticism, self-doubt, and tarnish a person's overall outlook on life.

With the reframe and R.E.C.L.A.I.M process, it may take days, months, or even years to fully evaluate and reframe your mindset. Learning to reframe and reclaim your peace of mind is the primary objective in this book. Some items from your past chapters may still have purpose and meaning for you today, however, holding onto things that do not serve you is where many people find themselves stuck. Our hope for each reader is to learn strategies to help evaluate, reframe and reclaim your personal space and peace of mind. This is your journey. *Where are you going? What are you taking with you?*

CHAPTER 11

THE FINAL TRIP

"I don't want my legacy to be containers full of stuff."
– Courtney Carver

Jennifer

Bringing the book full circle, we are going to end this book where we started it, talking about death.

Now that you have reflected, and hopefully evaluated some of your own items, fast forward to the end of your life. Now, do not feel sad and depressed. It was a beautiful funeral and you were surrounded by love. There were a few embarrassing stories you may not have wanted others to share but they brought a good laugh and a smile to your loved ones. Plus, you are dead now and you *finally* don't care what others think about you.

Your loved ones now have the responsibility of sifting through all your lifelong belongings you have collected throughout your years on Earth. What does that look like for your family now that you are no longer living? Is it messy? Is it stressful? How many days, months, or even years will it take them to sort and purge through the items in your possession? Are these items a reflection of what you truly valued in your life? Do the items left for your loved ones to sort through reflect the life you lived and the memories that were most valuable to you? Will your loved ones understand why you had over fifty throw pillows or two oversized bins of Barbies? Does your collection of handbags reflect the values you held when you were alive?

In your last days, do you want to be spending your time communicating to your loved ones the importance of the items you chose to collect in your home or would you rather spend the time recollecting joyful memories and time spent together? My grandmother told my mother, "I want you to fight over it when I'm dead." While it was a humorous way to deflect the responsibility of her personal possessions from herself, this strategy took years to complete. It was difficult to gather all three siblings together to go through everything and divide her belongings in a way that felt good to everyone. While the issues have been resolved today, this created more conflict than closure following her death.

How wonderful would it be to give your family direction in understanding the value and hopes for your belongings left behind instead of your family fighting over your belongings or feeling overwhelmed with what to do with all of your stuff after you have left this life? A legacy of endless boxes of stuff to sort through and make meaning of is not the most favorable legacy and responsibility to defer to your children and extended family. Only you can decide what legacy you will leave for others when you leave this life.

REFRAME & RECLAIM

Jennifer & Courtney

Now that you have made it to the end of our book, we want to thank you for coming on this journey with us. If you have started the **Reframe and R.E.C.L.A.I.M.** process, we want you to think about how far you have come and how accomplished you feel with the progress you have made on your personal journey. As you look back on your personal R.E.C.L.A.I.M. process, reflect on the following questions,

- How have you reframed your values and your relationship with your stuff?
- What have you learned about yourself in this journey?
- How do your items reflect your personal values in life?
- How much real estate have you reclaimed in your personal R.E.C.L.A.I.M. process?
- How did you feel relinquishing items in your space?
- How many boxes of items did you donate or pass on to someone, bringing new life and purpose to these items?
- How has the change in visual clutter affected your mental well-being?
- Do you feel different having more intentional and organized spaces in your home?
- How does it feel to know where your most treasured items are in your space and have a plan to ensure they are well preserved?
- How does it feel to have your most valued items displayed prominently in your space?
- How much baggage have you hidden or stored away?
- What habits do you hope to change as you continue your Reframe and R.E.C.L.A.I.M. journey?
- What legacy do you hope to leave for your loved ones?
- How do you want others to remember you?

We hope you have enjoyed taking this journey with us as we have shared our personal and professional experiences, perspectives, and advice. Thank you to all of our clients that trusted in us and our mission to share the Reframe and R.E.C.L.A.I.M. process. The clients in this book have brought our ideas to life by sharing their personal journeys and testimonies, giving readers the opportunity to witness the transformation of this seven-step process. As we have tried to illustrate, the journey of life is unpredictable, but you can take control of your home environment and how you hope it contributes to your everyday peace of mind and well-being. By reframing and reclaiming your real estate, you have the power to choose if you contribute to the calm or chaos of your life.

The American culture seeks a magic pill for weight loss or searches for a lucky chance investment that will ensure a large return on investment. But just like any diet or weight loss fad, if you have not committed to maintaining the process and reflected on your needs and systems, then you will be back where you started. Looking for a quick fix in life is tempting but rarely maintainable.

For those who have not reflected on their personal needs and committed to a system to maintain the functionality and balance of their lives, the work they begin will eventually fall back into habits that created the breakdown and dysfunction of their lives. To ensure that the effort put into a well-working system will endure, continued maintenance and evaluation must be kept at the forefront of the process. Creating a manageable and collaborative system will have more success than a process that is started but not followed through.

To be completely transparent, we, as the authors of this book have by no means completed our personal Reframe and R.E.C.L.A.I.M. journeys. For us, this journey is an ongoing process that shifts as our chapters in life and lifestyles change. As stated in previous chapters, it is helpful to take time to reevaluate and decide what to keep, discard, display, and store away in our homes. It may take multiple attempts in your journey to be able to evaluate some items in your space. Be gentle with yourself, but also be honest. If you choose to keep more items than you had originally anticipated, perhaps it is your mind and body telling you that you are not quite ready to make a decision about a particular item or collection of items. Give yourself time to attempt again in a few months. Reflect, evaluate, and reclaim your space according to your goals at that time.

Creating a system to maintain your space and evaluate your belongings may become more comfortable with the habit of the Reframe and R.E.C.L.A.I.M. process. The process can at times be stressful and overwhelming, however, the more you practice, the easier you will be able to decide what items hold the most value for you and what items you are ready to let go of at that time. This system can give you confidence in your own decision making and create space in your home that meets your personal lifestyle needs and functions. We hope the effort will be worth the reward in the end.

This book is written as a tool and reference guide to help you navigate your own personal belongings and the multifaceted challenges associated with stuff. If you have found this book to be helpful, we invite you to connect with us on our website or social media pages found below.

Instagram: @Reframe_Reclaim
Facebook: Reframe & Reclaim
Website: www.Reframe-Reclaim.com

RESOURCES FOR SELLING YOUR UNWANTED ITEMS

Use caution when selling or buying items online or on social media. Be aware that some sellers and buyers may not be legitimate. Do not give your phone number, bank account information, or credit card information on any social media platforms. Only give your address to a buyer if they must come to your home to see the items you have to sell. Ask a friend or family member to be present with you during any in-person interaction with buyers or sellers from social media platforms. Request buyers to pay cash or use an online pay app such as Zelle, CashApp, or Venmo for secure transactions. You can choose to meet in a public place such as a police station or well-occupied store parking lot.

Yard or Garage Sale
Taking the traditional route of selling your unwanted items from your home is convenient for many. However, the time it takes to prepare, individually price items, organize, and set up all of your items can be overwhelming for some. For some areas, city permits may be required. Some neighborhoods will schedule mass yard sales to increase traffic and advertise to the larger commu-

nity. You can easily advertise by posting brightly colored signs in your area or listing your yard or garage sale on social media or Craigslist.

Consignment and Resale Shops

Resale shops sell multiple household and unique items including furniture, vintage items, children's toys, and clothing. Contacting a consignment store near you to ask about the policies and processes to sell items at their storefront will give you the information you need, if this is an avenue for you. Each resale shop has different policies, percentages, and timelines for items to sell. This option allows you to support small businesses and your local community through resale, while also making some extra money for yourself.

Facebook.com
- Marketplace
- Buy, Sell, Trade Groups

Search for groups in your area by searching Facebook. Be sure to read and follow group rules and wait for approval by a group administrator. You can communicate directly with others in the group to purchase, trade, or sell items by comment or private messenger.

Decluttr.com

Selling electronics, media, games, and books is simple through this website. There is also an app for smartphones to scan barcodes and search for items or categories to sell. With a few questions to answer about your items, the site will give you an instant offer. They then send you the instructions and shipping label to send the box. Once your box is received, you are paid the next day.

Craigslist.org

You can create a free Craigslist account and create an inventory of items you hope to sell. Search for clear categories of items or list your items using the website categories. Be prepared to negotiate and haggle with some buyers and sellers.

eBay.com

This option allows some flexibility for selling items. You have the option to set a purchase price and bidders can bid on your item for a set period of time. eBay gives you resources to recommend pricing for your item based on other similar items. Opting to sell at a set price or using a best offer to negotiate and sell items more quickly are helpful strategies for eBay sellers. This site does take a percentage of each item sold but does reach a larger audience of potential buyers. For this site, you can choose to be paid daily or weekly.

Amazon Seller Central

Using Amazon is not only for purchasing. Individuals can also sell unwanted or unused items; however, using Amazon to sell items will also cost a percentage of the purchase price as well as a closing fee. For some, this is worth the hassle to reach a larger buying audience. Amazon also allows sellers to ship items individually to the buyer or send items directly to Amazon before items sell, allowing Amazon to ship the items to buyers.

RESOURCES FOR DONATING YOUR UNWANTED ITEMS

BetterWorldBooks.com
To donate your unwanted books, consider donating to this cause, to reuse and recycle books in lieu of purchasing new. This site boasts of accepting over 38 million books donated, 475 million books reused or recycled, and serving over 87 million customers.

CDRecyclingCenter.org
CDs were all the rage in the 1990s and 2000s. However, with the evolution of technology and digital streaming, there is more need for recycling. The CD Recycling Center of America accepts CDs, printer cables, ink cartridges, and more.

FreeCycle.org
This nonprofit organization is run by volunteers in local communities. The mission of Free Cycle is to help reduce landfill use. Organizations in your area can be found on this website.

Goodwill.org

This nonprofit accepts clothing and household items. The mission of Goodwill is to improve the quality of life for people who have barriers to employment by providing skills training and work opportunities. You can search for a local donation site in your area by visiting this website.

Habitat.org/restore

Habitat for Humanity ReStore accepts donations from the community to help build homes for those less fortunate. Donate unwanted or unneeded home items such as building materials, cabinets, doors, floor materials, and furniture to a good cause.

SalvationArmy.org

This nonprofit accepts clothing and household items. The Salvation Army is a faith-based organization aimed to serve the community and greater good to do better than good for the body, soul, and spirit. You can search for a local donation site in your area by visiting this website.

Smartasn.org

Sustainably and responsibly donate torn, stained, or unusable textiles including clothing, fabric, and rugs. To find a donation location in your area, visit this website. H & M Clothing stores are also donation sites for this organization.

Research your area's local nonprofits and other organizations for donation options. There are multiple retailers and organizations that will accept clothing and fabric for donation, resale, and recycling. Some retailers will also offer incentives for donations toward a future purchase from their store.

Several retailers are practicing the reduce, reuse, recycle motto. Retailers are beginning to sell gently used clothing in their retail stores online as well.

Below are a list of known organizations that will accept donations:
- Homeless Shelters
- Shelters for Domestic Violence
- Animal Shelters
- Local Humane Societies
- Wildlife Rehabilitation Centers
- Levi's Secondhand
- H & M
- ThousandFell.SuperCircle.World
- ULTA Beauty: Conscious Beauty drop-off site to recycle beauty product containers

TIPS FOR YOUR PERSONAL REFRAME & R.E.C.L.A.I.M. PROCESS

Now that you are ready to Reframe and R.E.C.L.A.I.M your own spaces, below is a list of materials, tips, and advice you can utilize to best prepare for your personal journey.

For Reflect
- A blank journal and pen to write down and truly reflect on the questions provided in the book
- A camera to take a before photo of your space

For Evaluate
- Empty boxes, bags, or storage bins to organize items into "Keep," "Donate," and "Discard" categories
- Masking tape or Post-its with a marker to label the keep, donate, and trash items
- A camera to photograph items you will be donating or discarding that you want to remember
- Extra lighting if you are photographing items to remember

- A light box if you will be photographing items and you do not want a background to distract from the item. Your phone may also have a setting to remove backgrounds as well
- You may also need an iron or steamer to reduce wrinkles in the background fabric of your lightbox

For Clean
- Any cleaning supplies you may need to get your space ready to assemble including disinfecting wipes, a broom, dustpan, mop, Goo Gone, sponges, paper towels, cleaning cloths, etc.

For Layout
- Masking tape or Post-its to label potential item placement for shelves, counters, closets, etc.

For Assemble
- A measuring tape to measure your space and appropriately-sized containers to fit your space. We recommend measuring the height, width, and depth of each space. If it is a deep shelf, be sure to measure the width and height from the front and back of the shelf because many walls are not perfectly straight
- A notepad and pencil or notes section on your phone to write down any measurements you need to bring to the store
- Any organizational containers or supplies you will need to create a functional and aesthetically pleasing space. We recommend buying extra containers or organizational tools in each size so you can create an optimal space

- Save your receipts so you can return any items you choose not to use
- Masking tape to label how each container or organizational tool will be used or what each container will hold

To Inspect
- A camera to take images of the space so you can inspect from various points of view
- Masking tape or Post-its with a marker to label areas you want to change and adjust

To Maintain
- A camera to take After photos
- A notebook and pencil or paper to write down guidelines so that everyone in the household understands and agrees on the system to utilize so that the space can be maintained. Buy in and accountability are key
- Once you have confirmed the space functions well for you and your family, you may want to purchase a label maker and convert your masking tape labels to an aesthetically pleasing permanent label

Share your Reframe and R.E.C.L.A.I.M. journey with us!

For a list of specific organizational items we love to use, visit our website or social media pages;

Instagram: @Reframe_Reclaim
Facebook: Reframe & Reclaim
Website: www.Reframe-Reclaim.com

www.ingramcontent.com/pod-product-compliance
Lightning Source LLC
Chambersburg PA
CBHW051537230426
43669CB00015B/2635